AVENUE OF ARMIES

A Brief History of the
Summers–Koontz Camp No. 490, Sons of Confederate Veterans
Luray and Page County, Virginia

ORIGINALLY ORGANIZED ON AUGUST 4, 1904, UNDER THE leadership of "Real Sons" Frederick Taylor Amiss and Arthur Ashby Grove, the Summers–Koontz Camp No. 490, Sons of Confederate Veterans, is a direct heir to the battle-proven veterans of the Rosser–Gibbons Camp No.

Frederick T. Amiss, first Commander of Camp No. 490 (Courtesy of a private contributor)

89, Grand Camp of Confederate Veterans (also known as Rosser–Gibbons Camp No. 1561, United Confederate Veterans). The camp was named for Capt. George Washington Summers and Sgt. Isaac Newton Koontz of the "Massanutten Rangers" of Company D, 7th Virginia Cavalry; both men being executed without trial by Federal soldiers after the end of the war in late June 1865.

Officially chartered on September 14, 1904, the original organization of the Summers–Koontz Camp existed for at least twenty-seven years before the camp was disbanded in 1931. In the fall of 1999 there was once again a strong movement made by descendants of the valiant Confederate soldiers from Page to reform the S.C.V. camp. Officially receiving its charter in March 2000, the Summers–Koontz Camp No. 490 was again reorganized and today continues to carry on the legacy of honoring Page County's Confederate history and heritage. The camp takes great pride in being part of the S.C.V. and its tradition of being a part of the oldest hereditary organization for male descendants of Confederate Soldiers.

The Sons of Confederate Veterans is an IRS recognized 501 (c) (3), non-profit organization. As an organization of the Sons of Confederate Veterans, the Summers–Koontz Camp No. 490 is a sponsor of *Avenue of Armies: Civil War Sites of Luray and Page County, Virginia* and, as a nonprofit, is dedicated to using a significant portion of the net profits gained from this volume to increase education and awareness of the historically rich Page Valley through enhanced historic interpretation and preservation of a number of the sites which are listed in the book.

Arthur Ashby Grove in his WWI uniform. Grove was Camp No. 490's first adjutant. (Courtesy of Ann Vaughn)

AVENUE OF ARMIES

Civil War Sites and Stories of Luray and Page County, Virginia

by
Robert H. Moore, II

THE
DONNING COMPANY
PUBLISHERS

Dedication

To my children
with the hope that they, too, will carry the spirit
of remembering things important from the past
and to
my grandparents and great-grandparents,
who passed that spirit on to me.

Illustration previous page:
"Confederate Spring"
by Charles Hoffbauer
(Virginia Historical Society, Richmond, Virginia)

The Donning Company Publishers
184 Business Park Drive, Suite 206
Virginia Beach, VA 23462

Steve Mull, General Manager
Dennis Walton, Project Director,
Anne Cordray, Project Research Coordinator
Barbara B. Buchanan, Assistant General Manager
Richard A. Horwege, Senior Editor
Elizabeth Bobbitt, Editor/Designer
Scott Rule, Director of Marketing
Travis Gallup, Marketing Assistant

Library of Congress Cataloging-in-Publication Data

Moore, Robert H.
   Avenue of armies : Civil War sites and stories of Luray and Page County,
Virginia / by Robert H. Moore II.
      p. cm.
   Includes bibliographical references and index.
   ISBN 1-57864-199-3 (alk. paper) 1. Historic sites—Virginia—Luray
Region. 2. Historic sites—Virginia—Page County. 3. Luray Region (Va.)—
History, Military—19th century. 4. Page County (Va.)—History, Military—
19th century. 5. Page County (Va.)—History, Local. 6. Virginia—History—
Civil War, 1861-1865. 7. Luray Region (Va.)—Tours. 8. Page County
(Va.)—Tours. I. Title.
   F234.L87 M66 2002
   973.7'09755'94--dc21
                                                                    2002152668

Printed in the United States of America

Contents

TOUR I

1861
Mobilizing for War
The People and Industry

TOUR 2

April 17–19, 1862
The Arrival of the Armies
and the
Hotchkiss Affair

TOUR 9

May 1864
New Market

TOUR 10

Early's Endangered Flank

TOUR 11

October 1864
The Burning

TOUR 12

May–June 1865
*The Summers-Koontz
Incident*

TOUR 13

*Reunion, Monuments,
and Remembrance*

Acknowledgments

AS WITH MOST BOOKS PERTAINING TO HISTORY, it is not a job for one person alone. Many different hands came into helping this book along; some in a major way, others in a minor way, but just as important.

First and foremost, thanks go to my wife and children for their patience while "Daddy" typed away at the keyboard. Without their support, this book would most certainly not have been possible.

Thanks are also extended to Donning Company, Publishers, an organization that has set up this very unique system that is designed to benefit nonprofit entities. Dennis Walton and Elizabeth Bobbitt have been wonderful throughout.

Thanks to the Summers–Koontz Camp No. 490, Sons of Confederate Veterans for giving sponsorship for the book. May they direct a significant portion of the funds raised from this book toward the very sites that are mentioned in this book, either through interpretive aids or preservation.

Thanks also to many different folks for materials, photos, information, and assistance including Randy Arrington *(Page News and Courier)*, Charles and Jo Ann Burner, Floyd Campbell, James E. Gander, the late Alfred M. Gibbons, John and Sandie Hammel, Scott Harris (New Market Battlefield), Marleen Hansen, John L. Heatwole, Greg Kelly, Phillip D. Lusk, Colonel Bill and Frances Menefee, Terrence Murphy, Daxx Moore, Edgar Poe, Mike Salvino, Tom and Linda Stumph, and Ann Vaughn, the Library of Virginia, the Museum of the Confederacy, the United States Army Military History Institute, the United States Military Academy, Virginia Military Institute, and the Virginia Historical Society.

This is also a book "in motion," so to speak. In the past four years, ten sites have either received interpretive help through Virginia Civil War Trails markers or Department of Historic Resources markers. Additionally, many of the sites listed in the book will have additional interpretive aids added to increase the overall enjoyment of the tourist in years to come. In many ways, the inspiration for this book has come through my affiliation with Virginia Civil War Trails. Mitch Bowman, the executive director, has been a great help in seeing that Page County received excellent support in getting nine markers in the ground to date. Additionally, thanks are extended to Bil Cullen, who was responsible for designing the maps on the markers. Demonstration grants from the Shenandoah Valley Battlefields Foundation have also been critical in providing 80 percent of the costs for Virginia Civil War Trails markers. Executive Director Howard Kittell has also been a major part of this project. Other critical players in the drive to show folks, in their own way, that, "yes, things did happen in Page County in the Civil War" have been, are, and hopefully will continue to be, Lori Nealis and the staff and marketing committee of the Luray–Page County Chamber of Commerce; Bill Vance, Mayor Ralph Dean and the Town of Luray; Judy Jewell, Mayor Clinton O. Lucas, Jr., and the Town of Shenandoah; John McNeely of the Ruffner House Bed and Breakfast; the former Page County Civil War Commission; Jane Fuller at Blue Ridge Community College; Don Sawyer of the Lee District of the George Washington National Forest, Julena Campbell of the Shenandoah National Park, Pat O'Brien with Luray Parks and Recreation, Mr. Robert Good of the Luray VDOT Office, Mr. And Mrs. Peter Baybutt, and Jeb Caudill, editor of the *Page News and Courier.* Yet others who have helped include Jo Ann Schaub and Violet Mitchell.

I also thank God for seeing me through such a wonderful project that is very much a part of my heart.

Lastly, with a work that has taken some fifteen years in compiling, I am concerned that I may have accidentally omitted some important people who have also made this book possible. If this is the case, my most sincere apologies are extended.

Introduction

THE HISTORY OF LURAY AND PAGE COUNTY IN THE CIVIL WAR is extensive and while the intent of this book is not to be the definitive work on the subject, it is an "abridged" version of activities that took place in the area and facilitates an "eyes-on-history" experience where readers will have not only the opportunity to read about various events, but also to see the sites where these things took place. Regretfully, only a select set of sites were chosen for the thirteen tours of this book due to their affiliation with the history of the opening of the war in 1861, their being along the path of the armies that marched through the county from 1862 to 1865, or postwar remembrance and memorial activities. There are many other sites in the area that were also impacted in some way or have a particular story that conveys an intrigue about the war.

Essentially, this is written for the tourist, both from afar and in the county itself. While many locals may see these sites on a daily basis, once you have experienced the driving tour, perhaps you will never look upon the places and the landscape as you had before.

In addition to the sites in the county, remember that Luray and Page County offer an excellent "hub" for battlefield excursions throughout the Shenandoah Valley. It is centrally located to nearly all of the battlefields in the Valley and, by following the routes of passing armies, several of the tours in the book act as an introduction to several battles in the Shenandoah Valley and Virginia. While no major battle occurred in the Page Valley, the strategic importance of the area is unquestionable as the veil of cover "under the shadow of the Massanutten" made the area an extremely desirable route of march.

Lastly, the book also serves as a tool for persons with interests in historic preservation of sites in Luray and Page County. After all, interpretation is one of the first steps toward preservation.

Both pages:
October 1854 pencil sketches of Luray by William Rupp.
By the time of the war the appearance of the town had
changed little. Note the image on facing page
reveals the site of the county courthouse
as well as the former site of Aventine.
(From *Page: County of Plenty*)

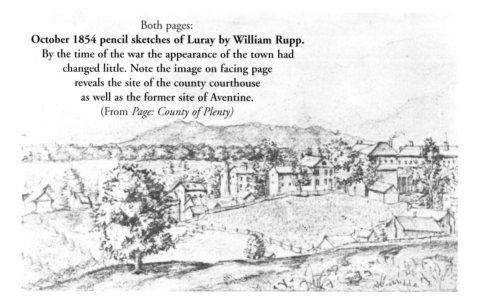

A Note to the Reader

THIS BOOK CONSISTS OF A NEARLY 300-MILE, 94-STOP/70-SITE tour of sites and buildings throughout Luray and Page County that were impacted in a particular way during the American Civil War. However, understanding time constraints, the tours are broken into thirteen different chapters/tours that allow you to pick and choose which one or more are right for you at a particular time. You have the option to follow the tours as they are written, or create your own tour by using the numbering system of the individual sites.

Please remember to be particularly safe and adhere to posted speed limits. Additionally, make certain that when you do read the book while on the driving tour, you do so only after you have made a complete stop in an area that will give you time and safety to read the information about the particular site at which you have stopped. As you drive from site to site there are also some other important things to keep in mind: Unless it is indicated in the text that you may enter a property or house for an additional touring experience, and since most of the properties/houses are privately owned, please be sure to respect private property.

There are stops at active churches. Please respect their privacy during services. There are stops that offer opportunities to walk through cemeteries. Please be considerate during Funeral Services. Use caution on the approach to and at some stops. You will be leaving hard surfaced roads to enter gravel or dirt lanes that are sometimes narrow and can be dangerous if excessive speed is taken. It is best to remain under twenty-five miles per hour on most of the gravel roads. There are a few stops that may put you close along the banks of the Shenandoah River. Keep a watchful eye that young visitors and/or others do not get too close to the water. Unless you stop in a recommended parking area at or near a stop, it is recommended that you turn on your hazard lights. If you have any concerns, please report them to the Visitors Centers at either Luray or Shenandoah. Your suggestions will be conveyed to the author and may be incorporated into future revisions of the tour book.

Peter B. Borst House, "Aventine"
(From the author's collection)

TOUR I

1861
Mobilizing for War
The People and Industry

Stop No. 1: 143 S. Court Street in Luray.

BEGIN TOUR NO. 1 IN LURAY AT AVENTINE on S. Court Street. The house was moved in the 1930s to its present site from its original location where the Mimslyn now stands. This tour is approximately forty-four miles in length and includes twenty-two stops at historic homes or sites and ends near the town of Shenandoah. It is recommended that the homes in the vicinity of Court and Main Streets be experienced by walking. Refer to the maps on pages 107, 110, and 111 for assistance in locating the sites on this tour.

The New Yorker that Represented Page County for Secession

PETER B. BORST HOUSE "AVENTINE"
National Register of Historic Places

Built circa 1851, this house was the home of Schoharie County, New York, native and secession delegate Peter Bock Borst. According to family legend, the house was named for the seven hills of Rome.

Known as a man of "wonderful force of character," in 1861, thirty-five-year-old Borst was selected to represent the county at the Virginia Secession Convention. Borst voted for secession in the voting on both April 4 and 17. Following the passage of the Ordinance of Secession, a public vote was held on May 23, 1861, and Page County had an exceptionally high turnout exceeding the 1856 presidential and 1860 gubernatorial votes. With a count of 1,099 to 4, Page's role was sealed tight with that of the Commonwealth and the Confederacy.

Following his return from the secession convention, Borst resumed both his practice as the Commonwealth's attorney for Page and supervising operations of his tannery business. The three-story tannery that Borst ran was well known as "one of the most flourishing establishments in the county" in antebellum Luray. However, as the war progressed, Borst realized that this representation came with a cost as Federal troops frequently seized his home for use during occupations.

A Family of Bold Defiance

BENJAMIN F. GRAYSON HOUSE
"COTTAGE ON THE CLIFF"

Built in the early nineteenth century, this was the residence of the Grayson family at the time of the war. Benjamin Franklin Grayson was not only a successful merchant but also the sheriff of Page County in 1861. As

Peter B Borst

Signature of Peter Bock Borst on the Ordinance of Secession for Virginia

Stop No. 2 is .1 miles north on S. Court Street; four houses down on the right to "Cottage on the Cliff," 127 S. Court Street.

Benjamin F. Grayson House, "Cottage on the Cliff" (From the author's collection)

13

Union Gen. Robert H. Milroy
(From *Generals in Blue: Lives of the Union Commanders*)

Stop No. 3 is .125 miles north on S. Court Street. County courthouse is on the left.

early as May 27, Grayson, along with Mann Spitler, Mann Almond, Nicholas W. Yager, Gabriel Jordan, and Charles A. Flinn, was appointed to a committee to carry out orders to appropriate funds through bonds for uniforms and equipment for any companies that were to be formed.

In 1863 Union Gen. Robert Milroy made the Grayson home his headquarters. Aggravated by the inconvenience to his family, ten-year-old Stuart Grayson plotted a child's revenge. Mounting a large stone in the middle of the night, he took the general's saddle pistols and hid them in the mountains. When Milroy discovered that his pistols had been taken, he was furious, but did not notice the absence of the boy and tie-in the possibility that he was the guilty party.

During the Burning in October 1864, the house was again visited by Federal soldiers. When a patrol went to the back steps of the Grayson's "Cottage on the Cliff," they were met by B. F. Grayson's wife, Caroline Siebert Grayson, a woman who boldly exclaimed that she would "lay on any Yankee who dared come up the steps." Impressed by her bold behavior, the patrol leader left orders for the house and barn to be left alone.

David Coffman Grayson, a son of the Graysons, served as a lieutenant in the Page Volunteers, Company K, 10th Virginia Infantry.

Temporary barracks and departure of the Page Volunteers

PAGE COUNTY COURTHOUSE
National Register of Historic Places

Completed in 1833, this courthouse followed the founding of the county by just over two years.

By the middle of May 1861 Townsend Young's company of the "Page Volunteers" had moved into an improvised barracks made in the building. During the two weeks that followed, the company of men drawn from all parts of the county drew family members into Luray, laden with assorted supplies, foods, and delicacies "which were served on a long table spread in the Court House yard."

By June 2, the company was ready to move out and join

the main army. Of the event, Lt. David C. Grayson later wrote:

> On that beautiful summer morning, when all nature was arrayed in her most beautiful garb . . . At the early dawn of day the reveille was sounded from the Court House by our drummer Joseph Bell as it had been suggested to this Captain that they had better march off early before the parents and relatives could get in from the country and thus avoid the scenes of sad partings, but this was circumvented, as no sooner had the early morning dawned than the people began coming from all directions and soon the street was crowded with the fathers and mothers and sweethearts of the young soldiers with heavy hearts and tears streaming down their cheeks . . .
>
> The company . . . marched to Chapman's Dam and there under the shade of the willow trees all knelt in prayer while Rev. Rippetoe offered a solemn invocation to the Lord of hosts after which all took carriages which were provided by citizens to take them to Winchester. From there they took the cars to Bolivar Height's.

Of the men in the company that would later makeup Company K of the 10th Virginia Infantry, Grayson wrote,

Early twentieth-century view of the Page County Courthouse (Grove and McKay Post Card, from the author's collection)

Pvt. Philip Monroe Printz. Private Printz was among those enlisted in the Page Volunteers in 1861. (Courtesy of a private contributor)

15

"all but 42 out of the company of 100, who marched off that June morning are scattered from Richmond to Gettysburg."

In all, Page County contributed some 1,300 soldiers, of which more than 10 percent never returned home from the war. In all of the wars combined since the Civil War, Page County's losses in wartime dead have never exceeded that of the Civil War.

Luray's Southern Poetess

FRANK AND CORNELIA JORDAN HOUSE "CLIFF COTTAGE"

Stop No. 4 is at 117 Court Street, opposite the courthouse.

Right:
Cornelia Jane Mathews Jordan
(From *Flowers of Hope and Memory: A Collection of Poems*)

At the time of the war, this was the home of Frank and Cornelia Jordan and two children by his first marriage. While Frank Jordan initially went off to serve as a member of the Massanutten Rangers of Company D, 7th Virginia Cavalry at the opening of the war, he was later appointed to his older brother's (General Thomas Jordan) staff in the western theater.

In 1863, while visiting her husband in Corinth, Mississippi, Cornelia wrote the poem "Corinth." Due to its "objectionable and incendiary" content, not long after the publication of *Corinth and Other Poems of the War* in 1865, Union Gen. Alfred H. Terry ordered copies seized and burned in the courthouse yard in Lynchburg.

Frank and Cornelia Jordan House, "Cliff Cottage"
(From the author's collection)

Ironically, a poem that appeared in Cornelia Jordan's first work prior to the war, *Flowers of Hope and Memory* (Richmond, 1861), included a poem titled "A National Hymn for the New Year," which differed greatly in viewpoint of the Union from her later controversial poem "Corinth." Ultimately, it exhibits the belief of many locals who were devout Unionist in 1860, and then later strongly Confederate after the 1860 election of Abraham Lincoln as president and the subsequent call for 75,000 troops.

Colonel Mann Spitler and the 97th Virginia Militia

MANN SPITLER HOUSE (POSTWAR "HOTEL LAURENCE")

Stop No. 5 is approximately .1 miles to the SW corner of S. Court and Main.

Born in Page County in 1825, Mann Spitler would become known as one of Page County's military and political leaders of the Civil War. Prior to the war Spitler played an instrumental part in the organization of the 97th Virginia Militia and by 1860 commanded the organization. Additionally, Spitler had served as a member of the Virginia House of Delegates from 1853 to 1858. At the opening of the war he was a successful thirty-six-year-old merchant.

Col. Mann Spitler House, later known as Hotel Laurence (Postcard from the author's collection)

Modern view of the Mann Spitler House (From the author's collection)

Henry F. Bradley served as captain of Company F, 97th Virginia Militia. (From the author's collection)

Stop No. 6 is directly opposite the Spitler House, on the NE corner of Main and N. Court.

Upon his return from service in the militia in 1862, Spitler succeeded Wright Gatewood of Shenandoah County and served in the Virginia State Senate representing Page and Shenandoah Counties from 1861 to 1865. Spitler also conducted a general mercantile business at this building during the war.

Originally enlisted from July 1 to July 7, 1861, the 97th Virginia Militia was made up of several companies of men from Page County, while a few companies came from nearby counties. Twelve companies (A through M) composed this organization. The 97th Regiment was one of eight regiments and one smaller militia unit to make up the 7th Brigade under General Gilbert Simrall Meem.

Available records indicate that the organization may have been disbanded in April 1862 by order of General Thomas J. "Stonewall" Jackson in response to the need to "activate" those men who were able-bodied and could serve in the regular regiments of Jackson's army.

One for Mosby and one for Texas: The sons of Nicholas W. Yager

NICHOLAS W. YAGER HOUSE

Built circa 1834, at the time of the war this was the home of Nicholas Wesley and Christena Overall Yager. Facing the front of the house, the left or west half of the building was the private residence while the right was used as offices and storerooms for Yager's mercantile business.

Nicholas Wesley Yager House
(From the author's collection)

According to a resident who had moved to Illinois, Abraham Lincoln looked "very much like" the merchant/farmer, Nicholas W. Yager "as to form and color." The Yager family provided two sons to the Confederacy.

Born about 1845, Francis Wesley "Frank" Yager was the youngest son to serve; first as the 1st sergeant of the Dixie Artillery and then later as a 3rd lieutenant with Colonel John S. Mosby's 43rd Battalion Virginia Cavalry. For details unknown, he was asked to resign his commission by Mosby on November 30, 1864.

The older son, William Overall Yager had a more extensive military career beginning as early as 1848 when he, along with Simeon Beauford Gibbons, matriculated at the Virginia Military Institute. Yager graduated fifth of twenty-four as a cadet lieutenant on July 4, 1852, and went on to continue his education, graduating from the University of Virginia Law School in 1854. By the opening of the war, he had moved to Texas where he was elected 1st lieutenant of state troops in 1861. By the end of the war Yager held command of the 1st Texas Cavalry.

View of the Gabriel Jordan House, circa 1900, then known as Mansion Inn (Postcard from the author's collection)

Thomas Jordan,
Page County's only Civil War general

GABRIEL JORDAN HOUSE
(POSTWAR "MANSION INN")

Stop No. 7 is approximately .1 miles to the east at 117 Main Street. The small portion of the original structure that remains is believed to have been the actual living area of the Jordan family.

Known years after the war as Mansion Inn, this house was built circa 1833 and was the home of the Gabriel and Betsey Ann Seibert Jordan family. Jordan was also one of several local civilian men to be arrested and placed in the county courthouse for refusing to take the oath of allegiance during the Federal occupation of July 1862. Stonewall Jackson's mapmaker, Jedediah Hotchkiss, spent a good part of the day here at the house on November 21, 1862, in the company of ladies who were "quite chatty."

Gabriel and Betsey Ann Jordan provided three sons to the Confederate Army; Captain Francis Hubert "Frank" Jordan, Captain Macon Jordan and, the only Civil War general from Page County, Thomas Jordan.

Born in 1819, Thomas had a remarkable life. An 1840 graduate of the United States Military Academy, Jordan graduated forty-first in his class that included future notables such as William T. Sherman (also a roommate), George Henry Thomas, and Richard S. Ewell. By the opening of the Civil War, he was a veteran of the Second and Third Seminole Wars, the Mexican War, and in the Steptoe War in the Pacific Northwest.

During the majority of his military career in the Civil War, Jordan served primarily as adjutant general to General Pierre G. T. Beauregard. For his role at Shiloh, Jordan was promoted brigadier general.

In addition to sustained service with Beauregard in Virginia and other theaters of war, Jordan was instrumental in recruiting a significant number of female spies, including Rose Greenhow. From Jordan, Greenhow also learned the use of a twenty-six-symbol cipher, and "began to exploit her connections with the prominent Unionists for the purpose of eliciting information that she then transmitted in code to relevant figures in the Confederacy." Greenhow was later credited with providing Beauregard with vital information that contributed significantly to the victory at First Manassas on July 21, 1861.

Confederate Gen. Thomas Jordan (From *Generals in Gray: Lives of the Confederate Commanders*)

Macon Jordan and the Massanutten Rangers, Company D, 7th Virginia Cavalry

Macon Jordan House

Stop No. 8 is located at 111 Main Street, to the left of the Gabriel Jordan House.

Pvt. Henry K. Emerson
Private Emerson was among the first to enlist under Macon Jordan's command. (From the author's collection)

The Macon Jordan House (From the author's collection)

Born in 1840, Macon Jordan attended Jedediah Hotchkiss' Mossy Creek Academy in Augusta County prior to the war. In late May 1861 he organized the Massanutten Rangers that later became Company D, 7th Virginia Cavalry. Mustered-in at Luray on June 2, 1861, the company was part of a regiment and brigade that gained a great number of laurels under the likes of Turner Ashby, Thomas Munford, "Grumble" Jones, and Thomas Rosser. Succeeding commanders of the Massanutten Rangers included Augusta County native and Jordan's classmate at Mossy Creek, Samuel Brown Coyner and George Washington Summers.

Though not re-elected to to command, Jordan was later appointed to the staff of Gen. Robert E. Rodes.

On November 20, 1862, while at home, Jordan met his former schoolmaster under amusing circumstances. While sketching the road near Luray, a boy saw Hotchkiss and reported him to the provost marshal "as having on blue

22

pants." According to the mapmaker, the boy "got Capt. Macon Jordan and some others to come and take me prisoner." Hotchkiss continued that, "When the Captain rode up he broke into a big laugh . . . insisting that I should go to his house. So I spent the rest of the day there and [then] the evening at Mr. [John] Lionberger's."

Jordan was twice wounded during the war, once while on General Harry Heth's staff in the opening fight at the Battle of Gettysburg in July 1863. On May 11, 1864, Macon married eighteen-year-old Mary E. Modesite in Page County and likely retired to this home as newlyweds. In 1865 Jordan sold his house and later relocated to Missouri.

The John Lionberger Family

JOHN LIONBERGER HOUSE

Built circa 1836, this was the home of John and Lavinia Seibert Lionberger. John was a successful merchant and was listed as a fifty-two-year-old gentlemen in 1860. John Henry Lionberger, a son, matriculated at the Virginia Military Institute on July 28, 1859. With the corps of cadets just after the outbreak of the war, Lionberger marched to Richmond and served as a drillmaster for forming Confederate regiments until June 1861. Like many of the corps, Lionberger then left as a student of the Institute

Stop No. 9 is approximately .01 miles to the east on the NE corner of Hawksbill and Main. The house has had significant exterior modifications since the time of the war.

Modern view of the John Lionberger House (From the author's collection)

23

Sgt. Martin Van Buren Gander
Sergeant Gander was a comrade of
Lionberger's while serving with the
39th Battalion Virginia Cavalry.
(Courtesy of James E. Gander)

Stop No. 10 is approximately
3 miles away, just off Bixler
Ferry Road/Route 675. The
Strickler House is .2 miles from
the pull-off, but there is no
trespassing beyond the
poultry houses.

for active service. Though he was listed as
having enlisted with Page's own
"Massanutten Rangers" of Company D, 7th
Virginia Cavalry on June 1, 1861, records
indicate that Lionberger was transferred to
Page County's Dixie Artillery in July 1861.
Though not while with the Dixie Artillery,
Lionberger was also listed as in command as
captain of artillery at Romney, Virginia
(now West Virginia) from September to
October 1861. By the spring of 1862
Lionberger was again in the ranks of the
Massanutten Rangers and was present at
the attempt to burn nearby White House
Bridge on April 19, 1862. By March 1863
Lionberger had transferred to Lee's
Bodyguard or Company C, 39th Battalion
Virginia Cavalry. He remained in the serv-
ice of this organization, with others from Page County,
until the end of the war.

First at Gettysburg! Company E, 35th Battalion Virginia Cavalry and Lt. H. M. Strickler

HARRISON STRICKLER HOUSE
National Register of Historic Places

Built circa 1790, the Daniel Strickler or Heiston-
Strickler House was the boyhood home of Lt. Harrison
Monroe Strickler, a son of Harrison and Louisa Strickler.

Late in 1862 Capt. John Henry Grabill organized
Company E, 35th Battalion Virginia Cavalry. Formed of
men from both Page and Shenandoah Counties, the organization included Lieutenant Harrison Monroe Strickler
who served as second in command of the company. Under
the command of Colonel Elijah White, the 35th saw most
of its service as a part of the Army of Northern Virginia.
Their wild charges with ear piercing yells often carried
them into enemy lines, and prompted Confederate General
Thomas Lafayette Rosser to give them the lasting name of
the "Comanches."

On June 26, 1863, White's Battalion, reduced to no
more than two hundred men, was ordered to take the lead

for an advance of General John B. Gordon's Confederate Infantry Brigade on the little crossroads town of Gettysburg, Pennsylvania. As the battalion approached the quiet town, Page County native Lt. Harrison Monroe Strickler and Company E, led the way, descending the grade to Marsh Creek. Immediately in their path was the Adams County Federal Cavalry and the 26th Pennsylvania Emergency Regiment. With a blood-curdling scream, the Comanches charged down upon the enemy, causing a route.

Following the return from Gettysburg, Company E, the same company that had led the way into the town, acted as the rearguard, and was among the last to cross the Potomac into Virginia.

Refusing to surrender at Appomattox, what remained of the 35th Battalion broke through the Federal lines in a wild charge reminiscent of their earlier days and was disbanded by Colonel White.

Colonel Elijah V. White
Commander of the famous "Comanches" (Library of Congress)

25

**August 1894 reunion of Company E, 35th Battalion Virginia Cavalry.
H. M. Strickler is in the middle row, 6th man from the left. Captain
Graybill is immediately to the right of Strickler.** (From the author's collection)

William Townsend Young House,
Calendine, later the home of
sculptor Herbert Barbee
(From the author's collection)

Stop No. 11 is approximately
4.3 miles away on Hamburg
Road/Route 766. Calendine and
the Museum are open to the
public May–October, Saturdays:
10 A.M.–4 P.M. and Sundays:
1–4 P.M. and by appointment.

The Merchant commander of the Page Volunteers
Captain William Townsend Young

WILLIAM T. YOUNG HOUSE "CALENDINE"

Built circa 1840 by William Townsend Young,
Calendine was his residence at the time of the war. By the
spring of 1861, fifty-seven-year-old Young was a successful
merchant in this neighborhood at Hamburg, just west of
Luray. Young also ran the nearby general store and coach
stop for the Burke Stage Line. At the time, the New Market
to Sperryville Turnpike ran immediately in front of
the buildings.

According to an early twentieth-century account by the
famous sculptor Herbert Barbee, "One morning," following the secession of Virginia, "while people waited and listened for the rumbling of the massive wheels of the four
horse stage, a little black boy walked in and took a seat on
a nearby dry goods box and began thumping its sides with
his rough rugged barefoot heels and modestly said 'Marse
Townsend, the white folks in Luray wants you to come dar,
fer big trouble is going on down de Valley.' Mr. Young, a

quiet, earnest man, listened but said nothing, but in due time rode to Luray and there called for volunteers to repel invasion."

Young was subsequently elected captain of the Page Volunteers, later Company K, 10th Virginia Infantry.

A number of years after the war, Calendine was owned by Herbert Barbee. Like his father, William Randolph Barbee, Herbert sculpted many pieces of art throughout his career. A fine example of his work can be seen in the Confederate Monument on Main Street in Luray.

The Page Grays and the Hite Brothers

DANIEL HITE HOUSE

On June 1, 1861, the "Page Grays" were enlisted under twenty-five-year-old Captain William D. Rippetoe. A Methodist Minister by profession, Rippetoe officially

Stop No. 12 is approximately 4.2 miles distant. When you reach Big Oak Road/Route 644, proceed .8 miles and pull off in the gravel entrance road, but do not proceed through the cow gates. Read about the Page Grays and the Hite Brothers. You can see the house by continuing on Big Oak Road for .05 miles where there is a swale in the road at the creek. The Hite House is to your right.

Daniel Hite House
(From the author's collection)

Captain Michael Shuler,
Page Grays, Company H, 33rd
Virginia Infantry, Stonewall
Brigade (From the author's
collection)

Stop No. 13 is approximately
4.4 miles away on Ruffner House
Road, just off of Route 340
Bus. N., in Luray.

mustered-in his company on June 19. It was later organized as Company H, 33rd Virginia Infantry in what would become known as the "Stonewall" Brigade. Other captains of the "Page Grays" included Ambrose Booton Shenk (killed at Kernstown, March 23, 1862) and Michael Shuler (killed at the Wilderness, May 5, 1864).

In all, Daniel and Rebecca Hite contributed three sons to the "Page Grays." William F. Hite would be the first to enlist and was elevated to the post of 1st lieutenant. Under his first trial of fire, William was wounded on July 21, 1861, at Henry House Hill during the First Battle of Manassas. With a wound to his lung, he died from complications due to typhoid four months later. David C. Hite, having transferred to the "Page Grays "in April 1862, was wounded at Second Manassas just over one year later, but recovered. Nearly two years after William's wounding, 1st Sergeant John P. Hite was mortally wounded on Culp's Hill at Gettysburg during the heated fighting on July 3, 1863. John finally succumbed to his wound on July 5 and was buried by David two miles north of the Pennsylvania town. For remaining behind with his dying brother, David was captured and sent as a prisoner-of-war to Point Lookout, Maryland, where he remained until March 1864 when exchanged. Almost six months to the day of his exchange, David would be the last of his brothers to fall, being killed-in-action at the Battle of Opequon/Third Winchester on September 19, 1864. A fourth brother, Isaac, also served throughout the war in a variety of units, was captured, and was the only brother not to fall in the war.

Mosby's Right Hand
Lieutenant Colonel William Henry Chapman

WILLIAM A. CHAPMAN/RUFFNER HOUSE

Built circa 1739, this was originally the home of immigrant Peter Ruffner. Prior to the war, William A. Chapman purchased the house. Three of William's sons, Samuel Forrer Chapman, William Henry Chapman, and Edmund Gaines Chapman, later served for the Confederacy.

A student at the University of Virginia at the opening of the war, William Henry Chapman first enlisted with a group of students from the University called the "Southern

The Ruffner/Chapman House
(From the author's collection)

Guards." Chapman returned to Page County after Governor John Letcher urged the men of the unit to return to their homes and "help organize and drill companies for the defense of the state." On arriving in the county, William began drilling the "Page Volunteers" and "Page Grays." Chapman declined an opportunity to serve as an officer in the Grays with hopes of forming an artillery battery. An opportunity arose when John Kaylor Booton organized the Dixie Artillery at Honeyville. Chapman later had the opportunity for assignment to John S. Mosby's command and was eventually promoted as second in command of the famous Rangers.

Of William Chapman, one mother of a Ranger later complimented him in saying: "It seemed to me he knew everything." At the end of the war, following Lee's surrender at Appomattox, it was William that offered the surrender of Mosby's men to General Winfield Scott Hancock. Complimenting Mosby's right hand, Hancock described Chapman as "important as Mosby."

In late May/early June 1863, William's brother, Sam, came home to this house to recuperate from wounds received while serving with Mosby.

Mosby's Fighting Parson
Captain Samuel Forrer Chapman

THE SAMUEL MOORE HOUSE

Built circa 1820, by the Ruffner family, this house was also home to the Gibbons and Forrer families. In 1860, Samuel Moore purchased this house from Samuel Gibbons. During the time that the Forrer family resided here, Samuel Forrer Chapman was born here to William A. and Elizabeth Forrer Chapman.

Before the war, Samuel had attended Columbia University and was listed as a minister in the 1860 census. Enlisting first in Company B, 17th Virginia Infantry, Samuel transferred to serve with his brother William in the Dixie Artillery in October 1861. Sam was subsequently elected to lieutenant and continued service with the Dixie Artillery until it was disbanded in October 1862. He was

Stop No. 14 is approximately 1.5 miles away, along Stonyman Road/Rt. 642. While a Civil War Trails marker on the right describes a stop on a later tour, look to your left to see the house.

Samuel Moore House
More commonly known as the Samuel Forrer House, this house was owned by Samuel Moore during the war. (From the author's collection)

on the list of artillery lieutenants recommended for another battery, though his destiny would remain closely tied to that of his brother William. Ultimately, Sam Chapman rejoined his brother in Mosby's Rangers and eventually held the captaincy and command of Company E in that organization.

Throughout the war, Sam was said to have "embraced combat as if it were an article of faith." Mosby himself proclaimed that Sam was "the only man he ever saw who really enjoyed fighting, and who generally went into the fray with his hat in one hand and banging away with his revolver with the other."

Booton's and Chapman's Battery
The Dixie Artillery

REUBEN NAUMAN HOUSE
"HONEYVILLE STORE"

Built circa 1835, this building was a residence of forty-two-year-old merchant/farmer Reuben Nauman, who ran it as a general store from 1851 to 1866 in the once thriving village of Honeyville. Throughout the war, the store served as a gathering place for soldiers being a crossroads of both the Luray-Staunton Turnpike and the Blue Ridge/New Market to Gordonsville Turnpike.

Stop No. 15 is approximately 10.5 miles away, along River Road/Rt. 650, near Alma. The Reuben Nauman house is at the intersection of River and Honeyville Roads.

Reuben Nauman House at Honeyville
This structure is all that remains of a once thriving mercantile community.
(From the author's collection)

In June 1861 a meeting was held here to discuss the forming of an artillery company from Page County. By June 21, under the command of Captain John K. Booton and 1st Lieutenant William H. Chapman, the last company to be formed solely from Page County was raised with a compliment of eighty-two men and was named the Dixie Artillery. By November 1861 Booton resigned his post, having been elected as a member of the Virginia House of Delegates. In turn Chapman was elected to battery command and would hold the position for the life of the company.

Assigned to General James Longstreet's "wing" in the spring of 1862, the Dixie Artillery saw service in a number of actions until it was disbanded on October 4, 1862, as a

Captain John Kaylor Booton, Dixie Artillery. Booton returned to Page in November 1861 to serve as a member of the Virginia Legislature. (From the Museum of the Confederacy, Richmond, Virginia)

result of the consolidation and reorganization of the artillery of the Army of Northern Virginia.

Foltz's Furnace and Union Soldier Underground Operation

CATHERINE FURNACE
National Register of Historic Places

Built in 1846, Catherine Furnace was named for Catherine Ebersole Forrer, wife of Samuel Forrer and mother of Daniel and Henry Forrer, iron magnates of the county. This furnace followed Furnace No. 1 at Shenandoah Iron Works and preceded Furnace No. 2 located along Naked Creek to the south. The 30-foot-tall main furnace is all that remains of the cold blast furnace and the once huge operation here. Due to the need for lumber to make charcoal, the mining of iron ore and limestone, and farming to support the workers, the furnace was part of an operation that covered 22,500 acres. During the war, Noah Foltz leased the facility and served as the iron master at the furnace.

Stop No. 16 is approximately 6.3 miles away, in the George Washington National Forest, off of Newport Road/Rt. 685. After entering Catherine Furnace Road, and when driving along the gravel road, be very mindful of oncoming traffic along this narrow road. Catherine Furnace will be .4 miles on your right.

Modern view of Catherine Furnace. (From the author's collection)

Ironmaster Noah Foltz
(From *Page: County of Plenty*)

In addition to continuing operations of the furnace in supplying pig iron for the Confederacy, Foltz was also a Union sympathizer and would assist Union soldiers to escape from the Page Valley, taking them up the trails of the Massanutten and into Fort Valley. At one time however, Confederates dressed as Union soldiers, revealed their identities after he had led them out of the area. Foltz was then arrested, but was released on bond to continue work at the furnace. His good conduct was guaranteed by the bond and the danger of trouble for his relatives if he were to continue his practice of providing an underground railroad to Union soldiers.

Solid cannon shot and, perhaps, a few cannon tubes may have been made here and/or at Furnace No. 2 on Naked Creek. Pig iron was transported by wagon from here to Tredegar Iron Works in Richmond where a much more extensive iron manufacturing and arms production operation was in effect.

The Iron Ore Industry in the Page Valley

FURNACES NO. 1 AND NO. 2 SHENANDOAH IRON WORKS AND SITES NO. 17-21

In 1836 brothers Daniel and Henry Forrer, in partnership with Samuel Gibbons, purchased land here with the idea of creating an iron works. Soon after, a cold blast furnace, known as Furnace No. 1, was built just to the south of the present location of Steven's Cottage. In all, with the demand of trees to provide charcoal, acreage to provide limestone and ore, and surrounding fields to provide sustenance for the workers, the iron operations here encompassed 6,249 acres. The Forrers later expanded the iron operations with the construction of Catherine Furnace (Site No. 16) near Newport and Pitt Springs, and Furnace No. 2 (see Site No. 18 on the county map) along Naked Creek. Furnace No. 2 was a steam hot blast charcoal furnace and included 1,014 acres. Each furnace used approximately an acre per day to sustain charcoal production that kept the furnaces in operation.

In 1855 the Forrers built their mansions that stood near the river along what is now Long Avenue. While it is unclear when the first mansion was taken down, the main mansion was taken down by private homeowners in the 1960s. It was made of brick imported from England and

Furnace No. 1 Anvil. The original anvil from the forge of the Shenandoah Iron Works. (From the author's collection)

Stop No. 17 is approximately 5.3 miles away, along Maryland Avenue/Rt. 602 in the town of Shenandoah. Continue to Steven's Cottage, a short distance to your right front. Though the cottage is postwar, this is an excellent site at which to receive more local information and read the descriptive information pertaining to Shenandoah. This stop is also very near the site of Furnace No. 1.

Stop No. 18 is along Naked Creek to the south but offers no historical vantage point for interpretation.

From Steven's Cottage continue along Maryland Avenue/Rt. 602, under the railroad overpass for .2 miles. Turn left immediately after the overpass into the cemetery. An anvil **(Stop No. 19)** used in conjunction with the original operations of Forge No. 1 can be reached by making another immediate left along a central road in the cemetery. A 10-ton steam hammer was used to shape pig iron, such as that seen in the corner of the cemetery lot. The anvil is not far from its wartime site and presently marks the grave of a person associated with the iron works after the war.

The Forrer Mansion. Built circa 1855, the Forrer Mansion was dismantled in the 1960s and little evidence remains of the house or the iron ore legacy left by Daniel and Henry Forrer. At war's end, the Forrers were land-rich but cash-poor and subsequently sold the business. (From *Shenandoah: A History of Our Town and Its People*)

From the anvil, take the circle road to the right and loop back to the anvil. Take the central road back toward the head of the cemetery and make a left and stop at the corner of Morrison and Maryland for time to read the story about the **Forrer Mansion (Stop No. 20)** that once stood about .3 miles across the road along Long Avenue. See map on page 106.

was a very elaborate work. Believed to have been one of the largest mansions in the Shenandoah Valley, it included 22 rooms and had inside walls that were twelve inches thick, while outside walls were eighteen inches thick. A July 1865 Hotchkiss' map (p. 106) reveals not only details about the location of the furnace and accompanying structures and surrounding wheat fields, but also two very large peach orchards and smaller apple orchard that went along with the mansion.

Col. Simeon Beauford Gibbons
(Georgia Department of Archives
and History)

A Son of Shenandoah: Simeon Beauford Gibbons

Col. S. B. Gibbons birth site

The son of Samuel and Christina Miller Gibbons, Simeon Beauford Gibbons was born in a rough structure somewhere near this spot. Later attending the Virginia Military Institute, Gibbons graduated, just behind classmate William Overall Yager, as 7th of 24. Beginning his postgraduate life as a teacher near the Willow Grove Mill at Luray, Gibbons later married Fanny Shacklett in Harrisonburg in 1855, and subsequently moved to that town and became a successful businessman and merchant.

Despite having entered the mercantile business, Gibbons did continue his affiliation with the military and served as captain in the "Valley Guards" prior to the war and was present during the imprisonment and at the execution of John Brown, at Charles Town, in 1859. In the year that followed, the 4th Regiment Virginia Volunteers was formed from the men of the area and Gibbons chosen for command. This regiment was among the first to report to Harpers Ferry at the beginning of the war in 1861. Elected as colonel of the 10th Virginia Infantry, Gibbons

Stop No. 21 is near the Anvil **(Stop No. 19)**. The Gibbons family lived near this site in a wood structure at the time of S. B. Gibbon's birth. There are no remains of the Gibbons House today.

served with distinction under Gen. Joseph E. Johnston at First Manassas. However, in the heat of battle at McDowell, Virginia, on May 8, 1862, Gibbon's rising star would come to an abrupt end. Though the Federal troops had been repulsed, Gibbons had received two fatal bullets. According to the history of the 10th Virginia Infantry, Gibbons "body was immediately carried toward the rear by members of the regiment. Gibbon's younger brother and acting aide, William S. Gibbons, rushed to his side but the colonel died just as he reached him. Gibbons died just seventeen days short of his 29th birthday."

Stop No. 22: From the corner of Morrison and Maryland, turn left on Rt. 602 and proceed less than a mile, across the bridge and turn right on Rinica's Corner Road/Rt. 601. Proceed carefully along this country road for approximately 2 miles and turn right on Shipyard Road. The Welfley-Shuler House will be down this road on the left. Though this may have been a postwar structure, John Welfley figured prominently in the operation of a black powder mill a little approximately one mile from this site, along the river.

WELFLEY'S BLACK POWDER MILL AND DISTILLERY
THE JOHN WELFLEY/SHULER HOUSE
National Register of Historic Places

Though the house likely dates about 1876, at the time of the Civil War, thirty-nine-year-old John Welfley probably resided in a miller's house near here where he had a good grasp of the various operations in this immediate area. According to tax schedules and other records, at the time of the war, Welfley operated a nearby water-powered sawmill, ran the nearby farm, and gristmill. A limekiln may have also been a part of Welfley's operation. In addition to this, by September 1864 he was also responsible for a distillery operation here.

Though a document indicates that a powder operation at the site may have been considered as early as 1857, by September 1862 Welfley began operating a powder mill to which seven local men were detailed from the Confederate army. Using a dam for waterpower, the plant also offered monetary opportunities for local citizens during the war. Digging the dirt eight to ten inches from underneath their homes, people would sell the dirt to the factory. Apparently the mill produced two types of gunpowder. The basic mix was composed by weight of six parts of niter, one part sulfur, and one of charcoal. Fulminating powder was also made but was of a different set of elements.

Modern view of the Welfley-Shuler House *(From the author's collection)*

Though it appeared that Welfley would have been well established in all of his works, he had been loaned a substantial amount of money in the 1850s and when it came due during the war, like most people, he was unable to close the debt. In turn he had loaned out over $11,000 that could also not be collected due to the war. By 1878 several factors had contributed to Welfley's inability to handle his debts and he lost his house and operations in this area.

Welfley-Shuler House, circa 1900 (Courtesy of Tom and Linda Stumph)

TOUR 2

April 17–19, 1862
The Arrival of the Armies and the Hotchkiss Affair

Begin **Tour No. 2** at Steven's Cottage (**Stop No. 17a**), on Maryland Avenue in the town of Shenandoah. Refer to the maps on pages 110 and 111 for assistance in locating the sites on this tour. This tour is approximately 21 miles in length and includes six stops at historic buildings and sites.

IN APRIL 1862 THE CIVIL WAR TOOK ON A NEW MEANING for residents of the Page Valley. Until that time, with the exception of small detachments passing through, residents of the area had been relatively untouched by armies on the march. Nearly a month after the Battle of Kernstown, on April 17, Union Gen. Nathaniel Banks pressed Confederate Gen. Stonewall Jackson's army at New Market with the intent of pushing him out and then deploying across the New Market Gap to cut communications between Jackson and Confederate Gen. Richard S. Ewell with his

Gen. Turner Ashby
(From Stonewall Jackson's Way)

division. Jackson prevented the Federal attempt and by April 18 sent his army on a forced march to Harrisonburg. By the following day he possessed Swift Run Gap near Conrad's Store (Elkton).

Jedediah Hotchkiss
(From *Stonewall Jackson's Way*)

To secure the area around Conrad's Store as a haven for reorganization and to allow time to plan the upcoming spring campaign, on Saturday, April 19, 1862, Jackson ordered his mapmaker, Jedediah Hotchkiss, to burn the three bridges: White House Bridge near Luray; Columbia Bridge at Alma; and Red Bridge near Grove Hill over the South Fork of the Shenandoah River in Page County.

Hotchkiss finds his Cavalry

SHENANDOAH IRON WORKS

To Hotchkiss' dismay, upon arriving at Shenandoah Iron Works, the mapmaker found several of the cavalrymen who were to accompany him in a state of drunkenness at an old iron foundry. The troopers consisted of approximately 150 men from Companies D and F of the 7th Virginia Cavalry. Company F (the Hampshire Riflemen) was commanded by Captain George F. Sheetz and consisted of men mostly from Hampshire County. Company D (the Massanutten Rangers) was commanded by Captain Macon Jordan and consisted mostly of local men from Luray and Page County. Jordan had also been a former student of Hotchkiss' well before the war at Mossy Creek Academy in Augusta County.

Riding on a few hundred yards to the Henry Forrer residence, Hotchkiss paused his "expedition" briefly in the hopes of sobering a few men from effects of the locally acquired applejack.

The "old foundry" likely stood just to the south of Steven's Cottage. The Forrer Mansion that Hotchkiss mentions was about approximately .2 miles from this spot, but was dismantled in the 1960s.

RUBE KITE HOUSE AT "DOGTOWN"

Built about 1777, this house belonged to Rube Kite at the time of the war. It was well known as a saloon and general place of public entertainment and the village was called Dogtown due to the nearby kennels. In addition to witnessing the passage of Hotchkiss' detail along the Luray to Staunton Turnpike, it was later a focal point of an engagement known as Somerville Heights in May 1862. The house was used frequently as a stopping point for staff officers throughout the war.

Continue down Maryland Avenue and turn right on First Street, just before the railroad overpass. Continue for .2 miles to Virginia Avenue and turn right. Continue for .1 miles to Second Street and turn left. After approximately .3 miles, turn left on Central Avenue/Rt. 683 and then right for .03 miles to Second Street. Turn left on Junior Avenue. Stay on this road for .4 miles, under the railroad overpass and this road becomes Shenandoah River Road/Rt. 683 (the "wagon road"). This road is also part of the original grade of the old **Staunton to Luray Turnpike** (ca. 1839). At the time of the war, though no longer an operational turnpike, it was the main entry point into Page County from the south.

To Stop No. 23, continue along Shenandoah River Road for .8 miles, under another railroad overpass to the just beyond the corner of Ridge View Lane. From this point you can see the Rube Kite House to your right.

Rube Kite House
(From the author's collection)

Stop No. 24 is approximately 2.6 miles away along Grove Hill River Road/Rt. 650. A Virginia Civil War Trails marker for Red Bridge will be on your left near the boat landing. The second marker at this site is for another tour.

Stop No. 15a is approximately 6 miles away at the village of Honeyville. The Reuben Nauman House is at the corner of River Road and Honeyville (see tour No. 1).

Stop No. 25 is approximately .8 miles away on Shuler Lane/ Rt. 614. The old abutment of the Columbia Bridge will be .05 miles on your right after turning on to Shuler Lane. Due to the undergrowth, the remains of the bridge abutment can best be seen in late fall and winter.

Hotchkiss Rides on to Red Bridge

SITE OF RED BRIDGE
VIRGINIA CIVIL WAR TRAILS MARKER

Having taken the old Luray to Staunton Turnpike from Shenandoah Iron Works, Hotchkiss and his detail rode about 10 miles before descending upon the first objective at Red Bridge. With no opposition before them, the bridge was reached. Sergeant S. Howell Brown, a cartographer and aid to Hotchkiss, was left at the bridge, along with a company of men under a Lieutenant Mantaur, under orders to remove the planking and prepare to set fire to the stringers. However, according to Hotchkiss' instructions, the bridge was not to be burned "until I should have time to reach the other bridge."

Hotchkiss' Detail Reaches Honeyville

HONEYVILLE

Continuing for about six miles along the Luray to Staunton Turnpike, the assembly of horsemen approached Honeyville, where Captain Sheetz was ordered to reconnoiter the Columbia Bridge. Reporting no enemy at the bridge, Hotchkiss ordered Captain Sheetz, with three men, ahead to prepare Columbia Bridge for burning. As Captain Jordan was among those rather inebriated, Lieutenant John H. Lionberger, from Jordan's Company, was sent ahead to destroy the White House Bridge near Luray. Meanwhile, the mapmaker "gave permission to feed the horses and let the men get out of the deluge of rain that was then falling."

Clash at Columbia Bridge

SITE OF COLUMBIA BRIDGE

Despite the rain, Sheetz' men set to work putting hay in the mouth of the bridge and began to set fire to it. However, their work was cut short when troopers from the 1st Vermont Cavalry arrived on the south side of the

46

bridge. Following a volley directed at Sheetz's party of men, some forty-four Federal cavalrymen under Lieutenants Franklin T. Huntoon and Charles A. Adams charged across Columbia Bridge and "put out the fire that had already been kindled."

At once Sheetz flew back to Hotchkiss' position at Honeyville, less than a mile distant from the bridge and announced the arrival of the enemy. Ordering the men to their horses and for Jordan to form his men, Hotchkiss found the Green Mountain men advancing rapidly along the road. With a round of shots from the Federals, the effect upon the Confederate cavalrymen was immediate and all but three or four broke "and a perfect stampede of them took place, the enemy pursuing for three miles." Hotchkiss continued in his diary that "Every attempt to rally was unavailing. Some actually threw away their guns, many of them their coats, blankets, etc." Reports from the Federal cavalry revealed that, in routing the Confederates, they "captured some prisoners, killing one man and wounding eight, some severely."

Despite a possible descending threat upon the Confederate troopers near Red Bridge, the Vermont men did not continue the pursuit however, and the bridge was successfully burned.

Though Columbia Mill was built as early as 1837, the namesake bridge did not come about until 1852. At a cost of over $277,000, the bridge was an amazing structure consisting of two spans of 145 feet each. It is believed to have been a covered bridge at the time of the war.

47

Stop No. 26: Return to the intersection of Shuler Lane/Rt. 614 and Rt. 340 Business, turn left. Continue for .5 miles and turn left on Leaksville Road/Rt. 616. This modern road continues to follow the old grade of the Luray to Staunton Turnpike. Continue approximately 6 miles to W. Main Street in Luray. Turn left toward Rt. 211 and then turn left/west on Rt. 211.

Rt. 211 roughly follows the grade of the New Market to Sperryville Turnpike (ca. 1848) which ran from New Market to Luray, through Thornton Gap and Sperryville in Rappahannock County, this road was the major west-east route through the Page Valley. Continue for approximately 3 miles and come to the Rt. 211 crossover to turn left onto Oak Leaf Road/Rt. 646. Once the crossing is made, stop and look into the private yard on your left to see Wheat's Boulder.

Pvt. Charles C. Wheat's modest headstone in a private cemetery in Luray (From the author's collection)

Lieutenant Lionberger's detachment at White House Bridge

WHEAT'S BOULDER

Like Hotchkiss at Columbia Bridge, oncoming Federal forces also surprised Lionberger's detachment of Page County men. However, Lionberger was apparently able to "front" or deploy his men to withdraw in a more orderly fashion from the field. As the Federal advance pushed the Confederates back from the White House Bridge, nineteen-year-old Private Charles C. Wheat of Lionberger's detachment was killed. Wheat earned unwanted fame as the first man killed during the war in Page County. Years after the war, local Confederate Veterans placed a boulder at the site of his death. Wheat was buried in the Wheat-Forrer-Kendrick Cemetery in Luray.

Aftermath of the Bridge Burning Episode

Hotchkiss returned to Jackson's headquarters at Capt. Asher Argabright's (the Miller-Kite House located in present day Elkton) to make his report to Gen. Jackson later that evening. Five days later, already angered by the overall lack of discipline in his cavalry, Jackson essentially relieved his cavalry commander, Col. Turner Ashby, by reassigning the horsemen to two of the Valley Army's infantry brigade commanders. Infuriated, Ashby submitted his resignation and immediately caused a rift in Jackson's command. Through some mediation made by infantry brigade commander Gen. Charles W. Winder, Jackson realized that such problems within his command could not be afforded on the verge of a major campaign. A compromise was then agreed upon wherein Ashby, though not officially given command of his men, would have the companies "detailed" to him and be allowed to lead his men if he agreed to tighten discipline within his command. Though the Valley Army quartermaster indicated that Stonewall had backed "square down," Jackson had, in fact, effected a compromise, retaining the integrity of his command.

Wheat's Boulder. This large stone near Luray marks the site of the first combat-related death resulting from military action in Page County. (From the author's collection)

TOUR 3

April 20–May 12, 1862
The Federal Occupation of Luray and Page County

Begin **Tour No. 3** at Aventine Hill **(Stop No. 27)** in Luray. This tour is approximately 34 miles in length and includes 6 stops at historic buildings and sites. The tour loops through the county and returns to Luray. Refer to the maps on pages 107 and 111 for assistance in locating the sites on this tour.

Union Gen. Nathaniel P. Banks
(From the author's collection)

Stop No. 28: Continue on to W. Main Street for .35 miles. Turn right on Rt. 340 Business/S. Broad Street. Continue for approximately 11 miles through Stanley, Alma, and across the bridge. Turn right on Shuler Lane/Rt. 614. Proceed past the site of Columbia Bridge for 1.5 miles. Slow down and look to the left in the field to see the site of the Elder John Koontz/Andrew Jackson Shuler House. The road you are now on was, at the time of the war, part of the old Blue Ridge/New Market to Gordonsville Turnpike.

50

Federal troops Occupy Luray

AVENTINE HILL
PRESENT SITE OF THE MIMSLYN

BY APRIL 20, ELEMENTS OF GEN. NATHANIEL BANKS' Federal army continued to roll into Page County and two days later, Luray was considered an occupied town. Federal troops holding most of Page County stood eye-to-eye with Confederate pickets posted along the South Fork of the Shenandoah River and awaited Jackson's next move. Upon Banks' arrival at Luray it was reported that "The people were greatly alarmed at first on account of the reports circulated by the rebels as to the treatment they would receive from us, but in a few hours they became quite reconciled to the presence of the troops."

Federal Troops Bed-Down at the Andrew Jackson Shuler Farm

A. JACKSON SHULER/
ELDER JOHN KOONTZ FARM

As Federal troops concentrated in the area around Columbia Bridge, the Andrew Jackson Shuler farm became a major campsite with no less than a brigade present at any one time through May. Prior to the arrival of Federal soldiers, the Shuler family hurriedly began hiding things that might be tempting targets for the arriving troops. According to a postwar account, the Shuler family made a hiding place in the cellar for the meats. In order to hide the route to the cellar, the kitchen table was placed as a trapdoor and proved a success in the concealment of meats. Additionally, three barrels of flour were hidden under the barn floor. Ironically, the non-commissioned officers decided to take over the barn as their quarters, necessitating a daily visit by someone in the family who would discreetly check to see if all was well with the flour. The Federal officers requested that they be fed in the large dining room of the home, for which the women were paid in gold coin.

As the Federal troops settled into their nearly month-long respite, local boys often came through the camp and played with the Federal general's twelve-year-old son. One

Koontz-Shuler House. The stone chimneys mark the site of the wartime residence of Andrew Jackson Shuler. (From the author's collection)

Union Gen. Jeremiah C. Sullivan *(United States Army Military History Institute/ USAMHI, Carlisle, Pennsylvania)*

day however, a fight broke out between the boy and a local boy by the name of Perry Dovel. According to Carroll Shuler,

> The soldiers quickly formed a big ring and let the boys 'go at it.' It so happened that Perry . . . was a real good fist fighter and it did not take him long to finish off his northern opponent. The soldiers grabbed up little Perry and carried him around on their shoulders as the champ. It was quite evident they did not like the general's son too well. After that whenever the local boys would go near the camp this young fellow would run out and shake his fist at them and yell' you d___ Rebels, get out of this camp.

Picket Duty at Columbia Bridge

COLUMBIA FORD

In early May, Jackson moved most of his army east over the Blue Ridge toward Charlottesville, leaving behind Gen. Richard S. Ewell's division at Conrad's Store (Elkton) to hold the Federals in the Shenandoah Valley. Union commanders suspected that Jackson was en route to reinforce Confederate forces at Richmond. However, they were unaware of his return to the Valley via railroad on May 3 and his subsequent advance toward Federal troops in McDowell in Highland County, Virginia.

As early as Saturday, May 3, Federal Gen. Nathaniel Banks began to probe Ewell's Confederates along the South Fork. Every day for three days, the 1st West Virginia Infantry would leave its campsite near Columbia Bridge and march eight miles upriver to near Dogtown, where it engaged Confederate troops in sharp skirmishes. On Sunday, May 4, the probe resulted in one Federal killed and one captured. On Monday May 5, the regiment was "surrounded . . . but faced about and cut our way out."

By Tuesday, May 6, the 13th Indiana Infantry began spearheading the reconnaissance efforts.

On the following morning, pickets of the 13th Indiana Infantry were attacked by elements of the 6th Virginia Cavalry and one company of the 9th Louisiana Infantry (of Gen. Richard Taylor's brigade), posted on the east side of

For **Stop No. 29,** Turn around and return to the site of the old Columbis Bridge, 1.5 miles distant, near Rt. 340 Business. Turn left on Rt. 340 north and proceed for .2 miles across the bridge to River Road/Rt. 650. Turn right and then make another immediate right toward the boat landing, under the bridge and loop around to look toward the site of Columbia Bridge. At times in the late fall, winter, and early spring, you can get an excellent view of the abutments from a point underneath the modern bridge, looking west.

the Shenandoah River. Subsequently, Gen. Jeremiah C. Sullivan, then commanding the brigade at Columbia Bridge, ordered Col. Robert S. Foster to deploy six companies from the 13th Indiana and drive the Confederates back.

Fighting at Somerville Heights and along the river

SOMERVILLE HEIGHTS ACTION SITE
VIRGINIA CIVIL WAR TRAILS MARKER

Foster had marched "about two and a half miles" before he encountered the Confederate "advance guard" immediately in his front "atop a hill." By this time, the 7th Louisiana Infantry, under Maj. Davidson Penn, was moving in the direction of the action along the river. Deploying three of his companies on the sides of the road, Foster continued forward along the road with the other three companies. Colonel Foster wrote:

> We found the enemy's force . . . to consist of two companies of cavalry and two companies of infantry, with one piece of artillery, which I afterward learned to be under command of Major Wheat of the Louisiana battalion. We drove him from this position, and continued to drive him through Somerville to Dogtown, under a heavy fire from our skirmishers, killing two of the enemy's cavalry and capturing a carbine and a sabre.

Falling back to Somerville, and then on toward Honeyville, Foster received a message from a company of the 1st Vermont Cavalry that had accompanied the Hoosiers, that they were surrounded and desperately in need of assistance. Foster at once ordered his men to "about face," and called up the reserve companies.

By the time Foster's men had reached Somerville, his Hoosiers were facing what he claimed to be "two regiments of infantry, and three companies of cavalry, at a distance of one hundred yards." Deploying his companies along the heights near the road, Foster's men drove back the skirmishers "two or three hundred yards on to their main body, which we engaged for a half-hour under a most terrific fire from the enemy." The Confederates attempted a flanking

Stop No. 30: Continue along Rt. 650 for 5.2 miles from the Columbia Bridge Stop to the Somerville Heights Civil War Trails marker.

Maj. C. Roberdeau Wheat
Major Wheat's Louisiana troops were the first to engage Foster's Hoosiers along the old Luray to Staunton Turnpike. (From *Gentle Tiger: The Gallant Life of Roberdeau Wheat*)

53

The men of Capt. George P. Conger's Company B, 1st Vermont Cavalry had to ford this portion of the South Fork Shenandoah River to safety, after the arrival of Foster's 13th Indiana Infantry. Conger was later involved fighting Confedrate raiders in the famous St. Albans' Raid after he had returned home to Vermont while on furlough. (Photo by the author)

maneuver but were countered by the reserve elements of the 13th Indiana. During this time the cavalry was able to escape by "swimming the Shenandoah River."

Losses among the 13th Indiana in the small engagement numbered twenty-nine killed, wounded, captured, and missing, including the sergeant major of the regiment. Col. Foster reported that his number engaged included 180 men. The Confederates who were captured were entirely from the 7th Louisiana Infantry.

A day after the fight at Somerville Heights and Dogtown, Stonewall made clear his disposition and attacked and defeated Federal forces at the Battle of McDowell.

Union Gen. Robert S. Foster (From *Generals in Blue*)

54

Evacuation of New Market and Luray by Federal troops

CAVE HILL/AREA OF LURAY CAVERNS

On May 12, 1862, Shields' army of about 10,000 began moving out of Luray at 6 A.M. From Luray, the long columns of blue advanced toward Front Royal. Ultimately, Shields' division would join Gen. Irvin McDowell at Fredericksburg.

Along with the troops moving from New Market to Luray and Front Royal was William C. Crippen of the 4th Ohio Infantry. Crippen wrote a series of reports for the *Cincinnati Daily Times* under the pen name "Invisible."

Once the column began to move toward Cave Hill, Crippen wrote that they made "a long halt for rest on Cave Hill," for the day was warm, the roads were very dusty, and

Stop No. 31 is located at Luray Caverns, 13.8 miles to the north just off of Northcott and Rt. 211 in Luray.

Skyline view from Luray
toward Cave Hill, circa 1900
(Courtesy of the Ann Vaughn
Collection)

Andrew Jackson Campbell
Campbell was a veteran of the
"Page Grays" and co-discoverer
of the Luray Caverns (From the
author's collection)

all gladly sought the shelter of a forest strongly sprinkled with pine.

Gen. Kimball and I made a pillow out of a knotty tree root and were lying there puffing our pipes and brushing off mosquitoes, when a cheer and a roaring laugh from the rear aroused us into a more stringent military propriety. The object of the general mirth was in the shape of a Shenandoah pleasure carriage . . . a hearse, a bona fide hearse, plain in construction but well aired, with numerous open panels on each side. Three men occupied the driver's seat and inside the hearse, squatted Turk fashion, sat two women dressed in their Sunday clothes. The neighborhood undertaker and his family were on their way to make a visit, using this, his only family carriage.

Andrew Jackson Campbell, a member of the local "Page Grays" infantry company, and one of the discoverers of the Luray Caverns, barely escaped a court-martial that would have led to his execution in early 1863. Having been absent without leave from November to December 1862, Campbell however, delivered a satisfactory excuse and went on to see the end of the war and the development of tourism centered on the Luray Caverns.

Kimball's Brigade passes through Luray

MANN SPITLER HOUSE

Later in the day, after following the hearse to Hamburg, Crippen regained the path to Luray along the New Market to Sperryville Turnpike and upon Main Street as his regiment marched through the county seat.

Wrote Crippen:

> While the brigade was passing through Luray, I observed an intelligent, well-dressed citizen sitting in front of his house, and noting that he was sensibly affected when the band struck up 'Hail Columbia,' I thought he would do to talk to. He was very talkative and here are his remarks combined into a little speech: 'This is a great army sir. You come down on us like the locusts of Egypt and can destroy us if you choose. This is a dreadful state of affairs in our country, brothers against brothers and fathers against sons, but my conscious is clear. I fought secession, sir, fought it with all my might, but when my State went out of the Union I felt bound to go with her.
>
> I had queer feelings when I heard the national air today; I love the old flag and the Union. What a great army this is. If you have many such, you will soon overrun the whole South.' When I informed him that more brigades would pass through the town tomorrow, he said the South may as well give up at once. . . I judge from various little incidents that there is a good deal of smothered Union feeling in the town. Some families gave bread and other edibles to the soldiers and would not take a cent as remuneration. At one house near the city a lady waved her cambric quite vigorously as the army passed. The genuine Secessionist, male and female, can be distinguished as soon as seen. They either have a hangdog look or attempt to speak defiance in their demeanor.

Stop No. 5a is .7 miles away on the SW corner of Main and Court Streets.

Union General Nathan Kimball
(From Generals in Blue)

TOUR 4

May 15–23, 1862
Stonewall Advances to Attack Federal Forces at Front Royal

Begin **Tour No. 4** along Shenandoah River Road/Rt. 683 along the grade of the old Luray to Staunton Turnpike **(Stop No. 32)** near the town of Shenandoah. This tour is approximately 26 miles in length and includes 7 stops at historic buildings and sites in Page County and Luray. The "Stonewall's Advance" tour concludes on the Luray to Front Royal Turnpike/Luray Road (Rt. 340 N.) near Luray. Refer to the maps on pages 107, 110, and 111 for assistance in locating the sites on this tour.

Confederate Gen. Richard S. Ewell (USAMHI)

The road from Luray to New Market Gap, circa 1910 (Asheville Post Card Company, from the author's collection)

Ewell Marches into the Page Valley to Join Stonewall near Luray

LURAY TO STAUNTON TURNPIKE

AFTER CLARIFYING STRATEGY WITH GEN. STONEWALL Jackson at Mt. Solon on Sunday, May 18, Gen. Richard S. Ewell put his division in motion from Conrad's Store toward the Page Valley, with the exception of Gen. Richard Taylor's brigade that moved on the western side of the Massanutten to meet with Jackson near New Market. Ewell would rendezvous with Jackson near Luray by May 22. Under a heavy rain, Ewell's men trudged along the Luray to Staunton Turnpike toward Honeyville and Columbia Bridge.

Under the Shadow of the Massanutten Jackson Crosses into the Page Valley

NEW MARKET/MASSANUTTEN/LURAY GAP

Less than two weeks after his victory at McDowell, Jackson was on the move to crush the Federal forces under Gen. Nathaniel Banks around Strasburg. However, in lieu

of a head-on advance confrontation along the Valley Pike, Jackson gave the illusion of heading directly to Strasburg, but made a detour at New Market, toward Luray. After a rainfall during the night of May 20, the following day, a Wednesday, dawned cloudy. As the day progressed and Jackson's army began to move along the New Market to Sperryville Turnpike into the gap toward Luray, the sun began to beat down on the long columns of men. Near the top, Robert Barton of the Rockbridge Artillery recalled that the "rising sun greeted as we reached the tip of the mountain, whence looking down its western slope a long line of rifles on the winding road glistened in its rays. The army in the far off curves of the road looked like a giant snake with a shining back, twisting its sinuous path."

Local Tale of a Brief Visit by Stonewall

JOHN A. BURNER HOUSE
"MASSANUTTEN HEIGHTS"

According to Works Progress Administration records based on the information provided by local residents, Jackson may have visited this house during the course of his march. Having had a lengthy chat while crossing the mountain, Confederate Congressman John Brockenbrough, who had come for a short visit with three of his sons who were soldiers with Jackson, may have also been present at the house. Jackson's party would have stayed only briefly during the day, as the general continued to ride on toward the White House Bridge and the village of Hamburg, at which place he arrived late in the day.

Jackson was also recorded as having left "a small riding horse tied under a large oak tree, just over the hill west of the house. John Burner, going to his mill that morning saw the horse, and as it was on his land he thought he would leave it there till night and then take it home. In the meantime Gideon Brubaker going to his tan yard situated in the mountain saw the horse also. He left the horse but returned home early in the evening and took the horse with him. Burner was a good Christian man and rather than have trouble with Brubaker just let him keep the horse although he needed it for the farm."

From **Stop No. 32** you will follow nearly the exact path of Ewell and his men as they marched toward Luray. Continue along Shenandoah River Road/ Rt. 683 for .9 miles. Turn right on Rt. 340 Business North and proceed for 1.6 miles. Turn right on Grove Hill River Road/Rt. 650. Continue for approximately 6.4 miles. Turn right on Rt. 340 South. Just across the bridge, make an immediate right on Shuler Lane/Rt. 614 near the abutments of Columbia Bridge. This is the old Blue Ridge/New Market to Gordonsville Turnpike.

Proceed for approximately 1.8 miles to Rt. 340 and turn right. Continue for 1.9 miles to Rt. 211 and turn west/left. Ewell actually went in the other direction, but the tour now moves to gain Jackson's entry point into the county. Proceed for 2.7 miles to Massanutten Gap and turn left into the parking lot at the National Forest Service Visitors Center. **(Stop No. 33)**

Stop No. 34: From New Market Gap, turn right on Rt. 211 East for 3.3 miles to Longs Road and slowly turn right, but loop back to face Rt. 211. You are now following the route of Jackson's men on their way to link-up with Ewell's two brigades. The Burner House, "Massanutten Heights," is immediately to your right front.

John A. Burner House, "Massanutten Heights"
(From the author's collection)

Stop No. 35: Regain Rt. 211 East by turning right. Continue for approximately 2.5 miles (across bridge) and make the crossover to the left and loop about to gain Rt. 211 West. Proceed for .2 miles. Turn right at the Virginia Civil War Trails marker.

November 1862 photo of Confederate Gen. Thomas J. "Stonewall" Jackson
The uniform he has on was the one that he shed for a new coat given him by Gen. J.E.B. Stuart (see Tour No. 7). (Courtesy of the National Archives)

Stonewall Runs the Gauntlet

WHITE HOUSE MARKER

Local Phillip M. Kauffman, a thirteen-year-old boy at the time of Jackson's passage in May 1862, recollected in 1926: "I was an eyewitness and, as far as I know, the only surviving one, not only of the crossing of General Jackson's army at the bridge at the White House . . . but also of Stonewall himself as he ran the gauntlet, with bared head, through the marching columns of his cheering 'foot cavalry.' His faded gray uniform with stars on the collar, his black beard and uncovered head, as he loped past the White House on Old Sorrel, are as fresh in my mind as on that day."

As the gray legions of men continued to follow "Old Jack" across the gap and under the shadow of the Massanutten, Kauffman continued his recording of the event. "I had two brothers and an uncle, members of Co. K, 10th Va. Infantry, and went, with others of the family, to see them pass, as it was understood they would not have time to stop at home, though only a mile distant. One brother dropped out of the ranks at Salem, west of the river, and came by home to spend a moment with his sick wife and young son, which proved to be their last meeting."

The White House
This Fort Home/Meeting House dates to the early 1700s and bore witness, as a neighbor to the old New Market to Sperryville Turnpike, to a great deal of activity during the war. (From the author's collection)

A Pause for Prayer in Hamburg

MAUCK MEETING HOUSE/MILL CREEK CHURCH
National Register of Historic Places

According to a Jackson biographer, the general halted late in the day at a "church to the east of White House Bridge." It is most probable that Mauck Meeting House in Hamburg is that church. At the time it did not appear as primitive as it now does. The present appearance is to reflect the way that the building likely looked at the time of the 1700s congregation that met here. Once here, Jackson

Stop No. 36: Return to Rt. 211 West and proceed for short distance to a point before the bridge and turn left and loop about to regain Rt. 211 East. Proceed for a short distance to again take the crossover toward Rt. 211 West, but do not turn left/west. Instead, proceed to Hamburg Road/Rt. 766, directly to your front. Proceed for approximately .75 miles. Mauck Meeting House will be on your left. It is open to the public by appointment only.

The Mauck Meeting House
Dating to the 1700s, this church was likely the one in which Stonewall Jackson prayed a great deal one night while his army prepared for an attack on Front Royal. At that time, it is likely that the church had clapboard siding, as well as a shake roof. (From the author's collection)

Stop No. 7a: Continue on Hamburg Road/Rt. 766 for .1 miles to the crossover to Rt. 211 East and turn left. Proceed for 1.4 miles to Rt. 211 Business/ Main Street. Turn left toward Luray. Proceed for 1.15 miles and pull-off to the right in one of the parking spaces next to the Gabriel Jordan House.

learned that Ewell with his two brigades was just a few miles ahead. According to the same Jackson historian, "Jackson prayed long and hard that night." Realizing that he held the upper hand in strength against a foe less than a days' march to the north, "he sought to curb the excitement with expressions of faith."

Throngs of "Angelic" Supporters in Luray

GABRIEL JORDAN HOUSE

By 6 A.M. the following morning, May 22, the Valley Army was again in motion. As the army passed through Luray, throngs of local women greeted the Confederates. Col. William C. Oates of the 15th Alabama Infantry recalled that as he passed through Luray, "I felt that I was marching to a carnival of death, through the portals of Heaven, and that the angels were singing and cheering me on."

Left: Capt. William C. Oates, Co. G, 15th Alabama Infantry
Just over a year later, he would be involved in a harrowing clash as colonel of the regiment as they went up against Union Col. Joshua L. Chamberlain and the 20th Maine in the battle of Gettysburg at Little Round Top. (From *The War between the Union and the Confederacy.*)

View east along Main Street from the Gabriel Jordan House, circa 1910
(Postcard from the author's collection)

"One of the loveliest spots the sun shines upon"

THE LURAY ROAD

Turning north along the old Luray to Front Royal Turnpike, Ewell's brigades took the lead with Taylor's Louisianans and Col. Thomas Flourney's 2nd and 6th Virginia Cavalry fanning out as the advance guard across the countryside toward Springfield, Oak Hill, Cedar Point, and Rileyville. In his command, Chaplain J. William Jones wrote, "As we moved down the beautiful Luray Valley, one of the loveliest spots the sun shines upon, past many pleasant homes and well-stacked farms, the people received us everywhere with the liveliest demonstrations of joy, supplied us abundantly with food of every description." John C. Donohoe of the 6th Virginia Cavalry commented "all along our route the loyal women of that beautiful valley, from the gray-haired matron to the fair, blooming maiden, flocked to the roadside to cheer us on our way."

While Jackson spent most of the march in the rear of his line, at one point he rode ahead to observe the progress. As Jackson rode to see Ewell's men, a soldier of the 13th Virginia heard "loud cheering in the rear, which came nearer and nearer . . . We soon saw that it was Stonewall himself, mounted on that old sorrel. We took up the shout and gave a hearty greeting to the great captain, who had come to lead us to victory, and the mountains echoed and re-echoed with the great acclaim."

While Jackson bivouacked that night at Bentonville, the long line of night fires of the gray-clad soldiers extended back into Page County. Brigadier Gen. Charles S. Winder's Brigade was, itself, only three miles from Luray when it departed at 5 A.M. on the following morning for Front Royal.

While the avenue to Front Royal was known simply as the Luray Road at the time of the war, it was actually the former Luray to Front Royal Turnpike. The Road was a critical avenue of activities throughout the war and offered the main entry point into Page County from points north.

Stop No. 37: Continue along Main Street for .15 miles to the stoplight and turn left on Rt. 340 North. Proceed for .375 miles and turn left into the Park and Ride area.

The town of Front Royal offers a 10-stop, 16-mile driving tour of the battle that followed this march through Luray and Page County. The Visitor Center is in an historic train station on E. Main Street in downtown Front Royal.

Col. Bradley T. Johnson, 1st Maryland Infanry. While paused briefly near Compton, Johnson received a dispatch from General Jackson to move the 1st Maryland to the front, and "in conjunction with Wheat's battalion" lead the attack on Front Royal. When Johnson read the orders to his command, the energy surged through the Marylanders inspiring them to move to the front with an "elasticity of step that elicited the admiration of the whole army." *(The Maryland Line in the Confederate Army)*

TOUR 5

June 1–15, 1862
*Shields Advances to
and Retreats from
Port Republic*

Begin **Tour No. 5** at the intersection of Rt. 211 and Ganders Drive/Rt. 646. Though the overall tour includes 6 stops for a total of approximately 41 miles, the "advance toward Port Republic" portion of this tour is 19.4 miles and includes 5 stops and the "retreat" portion of the tour is 21.5 miles and includes 1 stop. After a looping tour into the southern part of the county, the tour concludes in Luray. Refer to the maps on pages 107, 110, and 111 for assistance in locating the sites on this tour.

Capt. Samuel Brown Coyner
Although an Augusta County native, after joining with the "Massanutten Rangers," Coyner meshed well with the Page County men. Elected as captain of the company in the spring of 1862, it was said that his troopers "fairly idolized him" as their leader. After nearly 17 months in command, he was mortally wounded in action at Culpeper Court House in September 1863. (From *Confederate Veteran Magazine*, vol. 3)

FOLLOWING JACKSON'S ATTACK ON THE 1,000-MAN garrison at Front Royal, the Valley Army continued to press toward Winchester to attack the main Union army, by then in full retreat from Strasburg. Driving the Federal forces from Winchester, Jackson's success seemed complete. He had defeated and driven Banks from the Valley and alarmed the Lincoln administration. However, in response to Jackson's bold moves, a two-pronged Federal advance was to converge at Strasburg in an attempt to cut Jackson's line of withdrawal south.

Jackson marched south to escape. Two Federal columns followed in close pursuit—Gen. John C. Fremont on the Valley Pike and Gen. James Shields in the Page Valley. If Shields could march quickly enough to overtake Jackson's force in the main Valley, he and Fremont could unite near New Market and attack with a superior force.

The Burning of White House and Columbia Bridges

WHITE HOUSE BRIDGE

In order to prevent the Federal "pincers" from trapping his army, Jackson ordered his cavalry commander, Col. Turner Ashby, to destroy both the White House and Columbia bridges on the South Fork of the Shenandoah River.

As in April, the men of Company D, 7th Virginia Cavalry (the "Massanutten Rangers"), familiar with their home county, were once again called upon to complete the task that they were unable to complete less than two months before. However, Capt. Macon Jordan had moved on and Samuel Brown Coyner, Jordan's Mossy Creek classmate, had been elected to command the company.

Sometime after 11 P.M. on June 1, Coyner's company, perhaps accompanied by Jackson's chief-of-artillery, Col. Stapleton Crutchfield, began their journey from Mount Jackson in Shenandoah County toward Page and encountered "one of the most dreadful thunder-storms" half way up the Massanutten. After a brief pause "in the erode," the company pressed on under flashes of lightening that lit their way in the intense darkness. Coyner wrote "About half way down the mountain the storm was repeated. The rain fell in torrents, and the thunder rolled. And oh! The dark-

ness was so thick I could almost catch it in my grasp." At 4 A.M. on June 2, only one hour before the arrival of Shields' advance guard, the White House Bridge was in flames. Equal success was had at Columbia Bridge in Alma. Coyner recalled that "the Yankees" later "pitched their tents and planted their cannon by the smoking ruins."

Delayed by the burned bridges and the rising river, Shields was forced to abandon his plan to join Fremont at New Market.

Soldier Graffiti marks the avenue of march for Shields' Federal Division

LEAKSVILLE BRETHREN CHURCH

This German Baptist or Brethren Church was erected around 1846. During the Federal advance through Page County, as they passed along the old Luray to Staunton Turnpike (Leaksville Road follows the old turnpike closely), several soldiers from Shields' four brigades left their mark on the interior of the building. Among the scribes were

White House Bridge
Portions of the stone abutment of the wartime White House Bridge can be seen here, among abutment formations from later bridges at the same site. (From the author's collection)

Stop No. 39: Proceed along Ganders Drive/Rt. 646. After .3 miles, you will see remaining abutment stones of the White House Bridge **(Stop No. 38)** on your left. The distance from the corner of Rt. 211 and Gander/Rt. 646 to Leaksville Road/Rt. 616 is 1.9 miles. Turn left on Leaksville Road/Rt. 616; proceed for 1.1 miles to Oak Forest Lane/Rt. 644; turn right. Though it has been converted over time for farm use, the structure on your left is the old Leaksville Brethren Church.

The old Leaksville Brethren Church (From the author's collection)

Gen. Orris Ferry. Ferry's brigade was, along with Gen. Nathan Kimball's Brigade, ordered to remain in Page County in reserve while Generals Erastus Tyler and Samuel S. Carroll advanced with their brigades on Port Republic. (From *Generals in Blue*)

Capt. William C. Banta (who modestly transcribed: "best in the regiment certain") and five other members of Company B, 7th Indiana Infantry (Col. Samuel S. Carroll's Brigade); Privates Jacob Rosser and Jacob Bowers of the 14th Indiana Infantry (Gen. Nathan Kimball's "Gibralter" Brigade), Private Will M. Wix and two others from the 66th Ohio Infantry (Gen. Erastus Tyler's Brigade) and Sgt. Nathan N. Titus of Co. E, 67th Ohio Infantry (Gen. Orris Ferry's Brigade).

During the battle of Port Republic Captain Banta was severely wounded in the right shoulder by a shell. He later returned to duty and, by the close of the war, had been elevated to lieutenant colonel and commanded the 7th Indiana. At one point he was also placed in command of the First Brigade of the First Division of the First Army Corps of the Army of the Potomac.

Later on during the war, Privates Jacob S. Painter and Benjamin D. Engle of Company A, 12th Virginia Cavalry likewise gave their "Confederate contributions" to the walls.

The march from Luray to Columbia Bridge

LURAY TO STAUNTON TURNPIKE

In the days following Shields' arrival in Page County, the roads remained in poor shape. Capt. James F. Huntington of Battery H, 1st Ohio Artillery wrote that "the road was in horrible condition, at intervals there were lakes of liquid mud, which would engulf a mule bodily, leaving nothing but his ears in site." Shields' Division was hampered so much that at one point the supply trains were recorded as being mired and strung out for nearly 20 miles. "In several places we were obliged to cut roads through the woods from one hundred to five hundred yards in length to get round the before mentioned mud lakes."

Federals in Need of Shoes and Flour

SITE OF NOAH KITE'S "COLUMBIA MILL"

By June 7 Shields had made his field headquarters at Alma, near the site of the remains of Columbia Bridge. With the weather having cleared two days prior, Shields directed his attention to seeing to supplies for his men. Many were without shoes and equipment. Worst yet, food was in high demand. Capt. Huntington wrote: "we were suffering for forage . . . Jackson's cavalry had made a clean sweep of the grain left in the hands of the farmers, and our foraging parties returned empty handed."

In such desperate need for food, Shields put two flour-mills into operation at Luray. Collecting millers from his command, Major Sylvester W. Munn, the provost marshal at Luray, saw to the operation of the mills night and day and furnished an "ample" amount of flour. However, according to Shields, "our means of baking are so indifferent that we cannot march without hard bread. There are two other mills near Columbia Bridge which will go into operation as soon as the water falls." Though still in need of salt meat, hard bread, coffee, and sugar and 1/3 of his men without shoes, by June 8, Shields reported that too much flour had been produced and ceased operations of the mills.

Stop No. 32a: Return to the intersection of Oak Forest Lane/Rt. 644 and Leaksville Road/Rt. 616 and read about the march along the old turnpike.

Stop No. 40 is approximately 4.5 miles away off of River Road/Rt. 650 at the boat landing near the Alma Bridge. From beneath the modern bridge, you have a good view along the river and toward the abutments of the then burned remains of Columbia Bridge. Though you cannot see traces of the Noah Kite Mill, otherwise known as Columbia Mill, stood approximately 1/8 of a mile to the south (your left if looking at the river), along the east side, where you now are.

Stop No. 41 is 11.6 miles to the south and located just before Naked Creek/the Page/Rockingham County line. Turn left on Moose Creek Bottom Road. More recently known as Verbena, the present mill does not give an accurate representation of the much larger Price's Mill that was here at the time of the war. The first mill here was constructed by the Price family early in the 1800s. "Captain" Joseph M. Price, the second generation of Price family mill operators and the owner of the mill at the time of the war, rests in a nearby cemetery.

Milling operations weren't the only interest for Shields during his brief stay near this site. Accordingly, the Federals remedied the lack of a bridge and constructed a ferry across the river capable of transporting infantry, cavalry and artillery in addition to re-opening communications with General Fremont.

Witness to the closing days of a campaign

SITE OF "CAPTAIN" JOSEPH PRICE'S MILL

On June 8 the last of Shields' troops to pass out of the Page Valley en route to battle at Port Republic marched past Price's Mill, here on the Page/Rockingham County line. On that same day, elements of Shields' command, under Col. Samuel S. Carroll, came within a "breath" of capturing "Stonewall" at the town of Port Republic. Of the missed opportunity to capture Stonewall, one Federal noted "We had Jackson in a box with the lid on, but he kicked the bottom out and got away."

The Joseph Price Mill along Naked Creek near Shenandoah
"Captain Joe" Price is in the photo on the far left.
(From *Page: County of Plenty*)

However, Carroll's effort was greatly overshadowed by the defeat of Fremont at Cross Keys on the same day. On June 9, Shields' army was given a chance at Jackson's army at Port Republic, but also failed and was left to reel in retreat along the path by which it had advanced.

In the wake of battle, the 7th Indiana Infantry, retreated to and made bivouac in the immediate area around Price's Mill. With 191 killed, wounded, or missing, the Hoosier regiment suffered the highest number of casualties in Carroll's brigade and the 3rd highest number in casualties out of all of the Union regiments at Port Republic.

As Carroll's and Tyler's Brigades streamed from the battlefield at Port Republic, Kimball's and Ferry's Brigades, having been held near Luray in fear of a Confederate attack via Thornton's Gap, were rushed to this area to buy their retreating comrades valuable time and to repel any attacks from Jackson in the wake of battle. Within two days, Shields' defeated men would return to Luray, still awaiting supplies.

Modern view of the site of Price's Mill, known locally as Verbena. The original mill no longer stands but was replaced by the modern structure that is seen here. (From the author's collection)

As an option, if you have the opportunity to continue on to tour the Port Republic Battlefield, it is 15.6 miles to the south on Rt. 340.

To return to tour No. 4, from the site of Price's Mill, turn right on Rt. 340 North and continue through Shenandoah and on to Luray. **Stop No. 42** is approximately 21.5 miles away at the SE corner of Court and Main Streets in Luray.

69

*Every corner in Luray was filled
with dying and wounded*

Augustus S. Modesitt Residence

With the loss of over 1,000 men killed, wounded, or missing, upon returning to Luray, Shields' retreating brigades filled every possible house and street corner with wounded and dying. Despite the morbid scene, one member of the 66th Ohio Infantry recalled that "The female portion of the community seemed to enjoy our defeat—hugely! You could see them skipping from door to door happy as larks over the defeat of Shields' men."

Men of the 14th Indiana seemed to find some comfort in their campsite near Luray, even in the wake of defeat at Port Republic. One Hoosier wrote his "dear wife" while near Luray of what he referred to as "Beulahland:"

> Our camp today is in a beautiful grassy field, in the midst of magnificent scenery. Within three miles of us, the tall peaks of the Blue Ridge rise away up above the clouds, for the clouds literally hid the summits of many of them. Close by runs a fine stream of pure mountain water, affording an excellent place for dirty soldiers to bathe. I confess that such scenery has peculiar attractions for me, and sometimes in viewing it I almost forget that these lofty hills hide a hostile foe in their bosom, only a few miles away.

Reporting from Luray, though stating that his men had "fought like Devils," Shields gave proof that his men were in desperate circumstances. "What I want at Luray is shoes and stockings. I find that about half of my command is barefoot and foot-sore." In addition to the clothing situation Shields also gave insight in regards to his rations saying that "Hard bread and salt is indispensable to take us to Catlett's." As of June 12, Shields had been ordered by Gen. Irvin McDowell to remain at Luray until relieved by General Banks.

While Stonewall Jackson rested his troops at Mount Meridian before moving to Richmond, on June 15 Shields' regiments finally began breaking their camps around Luray and commenced the march to Front Royal.

This building is believed to have been built prior to 1828. General Shields is believed to have headquartered here after Port Republic. According to a local family story, Shields would swing the Modesitt children in the backyard. "He was especially fond of Elizabeth, later the wife of D. S. Stover, and gave her a pair of cuff bars."

Annie Printz House. At the time of the war, this house was the residence of Augustus S. Modesitt during the war. Union Gen. James Shields is believed to have headquartered here after the retreat from Port Republic. (From the author's collection)

Union Gen. James Shields
(From *Generals in Blue*)

TOUR 6

June–August 1862
Reconnaissance Patrols,
Reoccupation, and
Civilians at War

Stop No. 43: Begin **Tour No. 6** in the area of Overall (wartime Milford) on the Page/Warren County line. The tour is approximately 20.4 miles in length and includes 5 stops at historic sites and markers. The tour concludes at the Page County Courthouse on Court Street, Luray. The best opportunities to pull-off and read the description of the action here is actually on the Warren County side. Refer to the maps on pages 107 and 110 for assistance in locating the sites on this tour.

First clash at Milford

MILFORD/OVERALL

WEEKS FOLLOWING THE BATTLE OF PORT REPUBLIC and within days of the departure of Shields' Federal troops for Front Royal, Federal cavalry patrols were deployed to the Page Valley to find the disposition of Jackson's troops, whom the Federals believed might still be in the area.

On June 22nd, a detachment of the 1st Michigan Cavalry approached Luray and took reports from "the negroes that general Ewell was in Luray in force and that Jackson had sent to Richmond for reinforcements." Federal Maj. Charles H. Town noted, "Union people reported the enemy in force in and about Luray. At Milford it was believed that Jackson, lightly equipped, was moving toward the railroad to intercept Shields. A majority of people would say nothing of the enemy's position." Two days later, the 1st Michigan, under Maj. Town, clashed with Confederate cavalry at Milford in a "sharp skirmish."

On June 29 Col. Charles H. Tompkins, leading a cavalry contingent consisting of companies from the 1st Vermont, 1st Maine, and 1st Michigan, set out from Front Royal toward Luray. The mission of the hodge-podge brigade was, again, to feel for the Confederate disposition near Luray and report it to the 1st Brigade, 1st Division, 2nd Corps, Union Army of Virginia.

Late in the day, the contingent had probed as far as present-day Compton before returning to Milford. Saddling the horses by 4 A.M. the following morning, the Federals continued their advance upon Luray, leaving a detachment of twenty-five men of the 1st Vermont to guard the Milford Bridge. Earlier the night before, a detachment of twenty men from Company G, 1st Michigan Cavalry, had already established a watch on the bridge. Meanwhile, two companies of the 1st Vermont and seventy-five men under Capt. George J. Summat, went ahead as the advance guard to Luray.

Cavalry Clash at Luray

CAVALRY ENGAGEMENT MARKER C3

The first action opened between 8 and 9 A.M. within five miles of Luray, near Big Spring, as Corp. Barney Decker of Company D, 1st Vermont Cavalry, captured a Confederate cavalry vidette. As the small force moved on, two companies of Confederate cavalry, consisting of about two hundred men, were encountered, here near Yager's Mill, on "the hill about half a mile out of Luray . . . in a line just outside of the town upon the New Market or Gordonsville road." As the Federals moved in for the challenge, one company from the 1st Maine and another of the 1st Vermont moved in support another company of the 1st Vermont. As the columns of horsemen assembled, a charge was made, successfully dispersing the Confederates who lost two men captured. From the ranks of the Federals fell one man from Co. D, killed, and one of the 1st Maine wounded.

For **Stop No. 44,** from the Warren/Page County line, take Rt. 340 South for 11.45 miles. Turn right into the Park and Ride area to view the Virginia Department of Historic Resources sign and get a perspective of the action that took place near the hill just to the north in June 1862.

Marker for the June 30, 1862, Cavalry action (From the author's collection)

73

Confederate Gen. Beverly H. Robertson (From *Generals in Gray*)

Maj. Angelo Paldi of the 1st Michigan Cavalry continued the advance through Luray, and was ordered by Col. Thompkins to overtake the Federal cavalry that was still in pursuit of the Confederates. Moving out along the New Market to Sperryville Turnpike, at least four miles, Paldi halted and "perceived that our cavalry must have diverged from the road, as nothing but scattered rebels could be seen, and they far ahead."

While the expedition to Luray had gone forward from Milford, a band of approximately twenty-five guerrillas advanced upon the twenty-five-man Vermont detachment assigned to watch the bridge there. Approaching the Milford Bridge from the opposite side of the Shenandoah, the guerrillas turned back after observing the Maine cavalrymen moving up to ascertain the purpose behind the guerrillas' movement. By 9 P.M. the Federal force that had reconnoitered to Luray was back in camp near Front Royal.

Union Col. Charles H. Tompkins
(From *Photographic History of the Civil War: Vol. 10, Armies and Leaders*)

The Reoccupation of Luray

AVENTINE HILL

In yet another effort to reconnoiter to Luray, on July 21, under the orders of Federal Gen. Wilhelm August Friedrich Baron von Steinwehr, a hodge-podge brigade was put together for an expedition to be led under the command of Col. William R. Lloyd

By July 22, Lloyd's force held Luray and was encamped on the high ground immediately south of the town. The town was immediately placed under marshal law, with a company of the 6th Ohio Cavalry as the provost guard at the courthouse. Additionally, Secession delegate Peter Borst's home of Aventine was seized, after his evacuation of the place, and used as a hospital.

That same day at 5 A.M., Lloyd ordered a reconnaissance made to both the sites of the Columbia and White House bridges. Lt. Col. Gustavus A. Muhleck was to take the first expedition to the site of the Columbia Bridge with six companies of the 73rd Pennsylvania, four companies of the 6th Ohio, and the section of Capt. Julius Dieckmann's 13th Independent New York Light Artillery. At the same hour, Lt. Col. Ferries Nazer took four companies of the 4th New York, six companies of the 68th Infantry, and two mountain howitzers toward White House Bridge.

Muhleck reached his destination without meeting resistance. Nazer's expedition would prove different..

Stop No. 27a is approximately 1.2 miles away on Main Street, just in front of the Mimslyn.

Nazer's White House Bridge Expedition

WHITE HOUSE BRIDGE MARKER

By 9 A.M., Nazer's men reached the White House Ford, also without meeting resistance. However, upon reaching the ford, the Federals did encounter some "rebel cavalry, not more than 20," appearing on the opposite side of the river and "within rifle range." Having accompanied Muhleck's journey for about four miles, Lloyd decided to join Nazer's party moving on the White House Ford, and proceeded with his adjutant, Capt. Richart, and a small escort of cavalry. Lloyd elaborated:

Stop No. 35a is 3.6 miles away off of Rt. 211 West. Turn at the sign for the Virginia Civil War Trails marker near the White House. Though the marker does not describe the action of this date, the view from this point offers a good perspective of the action that took place just to the west

Capt. Roger Preston Chew
On July 24, a scouting party consisting of the 12th Virginia Cavalry and Capt. Roger Preston Chew's Ashby Artillery probed the Federals in the Page Valley. Crossing the New Market Gap early in the morning, the scouting party arrived near White House Bridge and quietly observed Federal pickets at that point. Unlimbering one gun, Gunner George M. Neese recalled that "we landed a twelve-pound shell right in the midst of them, which was a regular astonisher from the way in which the Yanks, in the twinkling of an eye, scattered." (National Archives)

Stop No. 3a is located approximately 4.1 miles away on S. Court Street.

We learned that 15 rebel cavalry had crossed the ford yesterday morning and recrossed about 9 o'clock; that about 40 cavalry crossed the night of the 20th and recrossed about 2 the next morning. We know that this party rode through the town of Luray and back the same night, shouting for Jeff Davis, but committing no other indiscretion.

Reaching the ford shortly after Nazer's men had arrived there, Lloyd continued to comment that ". . . A few shots were exchanged with the rebel cavalry, but a shot or two from the howitzers started their party back toward the gap." Concluding that the area around Luray was clear of any "rebel force of any description," Lloyd figured that the opposing force was no more than four or five companies that used Harrisonburg as their base of operations to New Market and into the Page Valley. Nevertheless, Lloyd would continue his stay in Luray for a while, establishing his own base of operations to send patrols "southward daily."

General Pope's Harsh Orders and Private Citizens of Luray

PAGE COUNTY COURT HOUSE

During the occupation of Luray, Gen. John Pope, now in command of the Federal Army of Virginia, issued two highly aggravating general orders. General Order No. 5 directed the men of the army to "subsist upon the country." After giving vouchers for seized provisions, there was the guarantee that reimbursement would come following the war. The downside to the order was that the person making the claim had to give sufficient testimony that they had been loyal citizens to the United States since the date of the voucher. Many voucher holders, even those who later testified, were not granted cash reimbursement. Furthermore, General Order No. 5 opened the Valley wide to seizures of grain, meat, and crops.

General Order No. 11 promised even greater despair for the citizens of Virginia. In it Pope's instructions were to "take up all active sympathizers, and either hold them as prisoners or put them beyond our lines. Handle that class without gloves, and take their property for public use."

Capturing sympathizers or disloyal citizens was not clearly defined and left the majority of the population fair game to the order. If the citizen had been disloyal, but was willing to take the oath of allegiance, the citizen could "remain at their homes and pursue in good faith their accustomed avocations." According to issues of the summer's *New York Times,* Page County was quickly affected as Gen. Franz Sigel's men rounded

Page County Court House, circa 1900 (Ann Vaughn Collection.)

up all male citizens of Luray and placed them in the courthouse for a time. Though none of the Luray inhabitants were sent South, Gen. Robert Milroy, headquartered in Sperryville, enforced the order with more zeal in Rappahannock County and sent at least eleven citizens out of the homes and out of "Federal lines."

One of the men held in Luray was the father of General Jordan, Gabriel Jordan. On August 7, 1862, Gen. Thomas Jordan, stationed in the western theater of war, sent a communiqué to General Beauregard and mentioned his infuriation over the latest situation in Page. Wrote Jordan, "The war is rapidly drifting to the black-flag phase. We cannot escape it if the new system prescribed in Pope's orders, and already inaugurated in my native county (Page) and village (Luray) is not stopped. We must accept the gauntlet thrown to us—accept the war as tendered us, and the sooner the better." Jordan also referred to Pope as "a modern imitation of the course of Attila, the Hun."

Union Gen. Franz Sigel (From *Generals in Blue*)

TOUR 7

November 1862
*Stonewall's Last Glimpse
of the Valley*

Begin **Tour No. 7** at the Page/
Shenandoah County line (**Stop
No. 33a**) at the Virginia Civil
War Trails marker in Massanut-
ten/New Market Gap. This tour is
approximately 16 miles in length
and includes 7 stops at historic
sites and buildings. This tour follows Stonewall Jackson's last
march out of the Shenandoah
Valley and along most of the
exact path. The tour concludes at
Red Gate Road, just over a mile
from where Jackson spent his last
night in the Valley near the village of Mauck. There is also an
optional site that can be reached
along the Skyline Drive. Refer to
the maps on pages 110 and 111
for assistance in locating the sites
on this tour.

FOLLOWING THE DRAMA INVOLVED WITH THE FEDERAL occupation in July, the following months were tranquil in comparison. While Confederate Gen. Robert E. Lee made his advance across the Maryland line to battle at Sharpsburg, Luray bore witness to the passing supply trains en route to Winchester. In late October/early November, Milford and Luray were temporary hosts to two brigades from Confederate Gen. John Bell Hood's division. Many of the men in the two brigades were suffering from smallpox and were ordered across the Blue Ridge to Madison and then the receiving hospital at Gordonsville.

By late November the situation near Fredericksburg grew critical. There, under Gen. Robert E. Lee, the bulk of the Army of Northern Virginia stood poised awaiting a contest with opposing Federal forces. However, Stonewall Jackson was in Winchester, where his "wing" of the Army of Northern Virginia had been since the battle of Sharpsburg. On November 22 Jackson's force of over 26,000 men began to move out of Winchester and south along the Valley Turnpike. Making its way up the snow-covered Valley, Jackson's force maneuvered through New Market and toward New Market Gap (also known as Luray Gap, Massanutten Gap and Page Pass) before proceeding across the Page Valley, and across the Blue Ridge to unite with Lee.

Jackson's 2nd Corps Established

NEW MARKET/MASSANUTTEN/LURAY GAP VIRGINIA CIVIL WAR TRAILS MARKER

On reaching a point atop Massanutten Mountain, sometime late in the evening of November 23, Jackson took the rare opportunity to rest and make camp. In the brisk air of the following morning, as his staff admired a commanding view of the Page Valley below, Jackson emerged from his tent and unintentionally prompted his staff to redirect their awe upon the old hero of Manassas. Having recently been promoted to lieutenant general and wearing a new coat given him by General J.E.B. Stuart, a tall hat purchased by his mapmaker Jedediah Hotchkiss, and a captured sword donated by a cavalryman, Jackson ignored the stares and boldly announced to his staff,

Page Valley from atop
Massanutten Mountain at
New Market Gap. The same
spot was also known as Luray
Gap and Massanutten Gap or
Page Pass during the war.
(From the author's collection)

A glimpse into the past.
The old grade of the
Gordonsville/Blue Ridge
Turnpike, circa 1930.
(Marken and Bielfeld Inc.
Postcard, from the author's
collection)

"Young gentlemen, this is no longer the headquarters of the Army of the Valley, but of the Second Corps of the Army of Northern Virginia."

To **Stop No. 45**, proceed along Rt. 211 East 2.7 miles to Rt. 211 and Rt. 340. Turn right on Rt. 340 South. Travel for 1.9 miles. Turn left on Shuler Lane/Rt. 614. This road is part of the original Blue Ridge/New Market to Gordonsville Turnpike. Continue for 1.8 miles to the site of the Columbia Bridge abutments.

BLUE RIDGE/NEW MARKET TO GORDONSVILLE TURNPIKE

Through an act of 1848 this turnpike was officially initiated in 1850. It ran from the eastern base of Massanutten Gap and intersected with the New Market to Sperryville Turnpike. In considering the modern roads, the pike ran from the intersection of present Rt. 211 and SR 615 to Shuler Lane (SR 614) to Alma and along River Road (SR 650) to Honeyville; Honeyville Road (SR 638) to Marksville (Stanley), along Chapel Road/Marksville Road (SR 611) through Mauck, on to Hawksbill Village and across the Blue Ridge at Fishers Gap. The pike was frequently used throughout the war.

Seal of the Blue Ridge Turnpike Company. (Library of Virginia)

A cold transit across Columbia Ford

COLUMBIA FORD

To **Stop No. 29a**, continue .5 miles and turn left on Rt. 340. Proceed across the bridge, and turn right on River Road/Rt. 650; then another immediate right toward the boat landing.

The march continued to progress for the next several days down the Luray to Sperryville Turnpike until it met with the Blue Ridge Turnpike just at the base of the mountain and made an abrupt right. For miles, the long line of

gray-clad soldiers progressed until reaching Columbia Ford. With the bridge having been burned only five months before, the men either used the ferry or took advantage of a makeshift pontoon bridge that may have crossed the site.

To the Page County soldiers among Jackson's Corps, the march through the home county was a great opportunity for furloughs. Having secured "permission for the entire company to go home" on November 23, Captain Michael Shuler of Company H, 33rd Virginia Infantry ("Page Grays") did not rejoin his regiment until November 27 in Madison County. The next two days, Shuler, along with his parents went down to the river to watch the men continue to cross. Private John P. Louderback of Company I, 10th Virginia Infantry ("Riverton Invincibles") determined to "go home and stay at home for several days" by November 23. Finding "all well at home" on November 24, like many civilian residents of the area, he went down to the site of Columbia Bridge to see "our regt Pass over, though it had Done passed before I got there." On the following day, Louderback went down to "see A.P. Hill's Division pass over. They did not all pass over to Day." Finally, at noon on

Mt. Hope. Jackson spent his last night in the Shenandoah Valley somewhere between Mt. Hope, the stage stop along the old turnpike to Fisher's Gap, and the village of Mauck, just to the east. (From the author's collection)

81

November 27, Louderback witnessed "the rear of the Army pass along" with about "sixty prisoners with them."

The four-day event proved significant for locals as having been the largest single assembly of soldiers to pass through Page County at any one time during the war.

Temperance in the Ranks

GRAVES' CHAPEL
VIRGINIA CIVIL WAR TRAILS MARKER

To **Stop No. 46**, turn right on River Road/Rt. 650 then .7 miles. Turn left on Honeyville Road/Rt. 638. Continue for 3.1 miles; the road becomes Judy Lane for a few yards; turn left onto Honeyville Road. Proceed for .45 miles to Rt. 340/Main Street in Stanley. Turn right on Rt. 340 North and continue .55 miles. Turn right on Chapel Road/Rt. 611. Proceed for .4 miles to the Virginia Civil War Trails marker to the left. Turn in at Graves' Chapel.

After crossing the South Fork of the Shenandoah River at Columbia Ford, Stonewall and his Second Corps continued along the Blue Ridge Turnpike, past Honeyville and past this church. It was also in the area around Marksville, perhaps just down the road as the old turnpike crossed the Hawksbill Creek, as recollected by Jacob H. Coffman, a local thirteen-year-old boy at the time, that "a barrel of whiskey was opened and each soldier was offered a drink as he passed, some however refused. Of course Coffman could not see but a small part of the army and that part was thus treated. This was a very delightful place for a camp as a clear mountain stream of water flows by the side of the road."

Stonewall's Last Night in the Valley

VILLAGE OF MAUCK

To **Stop No. 48**, turn left on Chapel Road/Rt. 611 and continue 1.6 miles (this becomes Marksville Road/Rt. 611). Slow down to view Mount Hope on your left (**Stop No. 47**). This was said to be a stage stop even before the turnpike came into existence. Somewhere between this point and the village of Mauck, Stonewall Jackson spent his last night in the Shenandoah Valley. Continue for 1.2 miles to the village of Mauck.

In his diary entry for Monday, November 24, mapmaker Jedediah Hotchkiss wrote: "The General went across the Massanutten Mt., from New Market, then, via Columbia Bridge, across the Shenandoah, and to within a mile of the village of Hawksbill, on Hawksbill Creek, on the road to Madison C.H. (Williamson made a sketch of Gen. J., on a log, in the rain, which he gave me. He had on the soft hat I bought for him.)" While Hotchkiss may have given a general location of Jackson's last night in the Page Valley, the village of Mauck is almost exactly one mile below the village of Hawksbill. Jackson bivouacked overnight somewhere in these surrounding fields, before marching across the Blue Ridge near Fishers Gap on the following day.

Stonewall's Last Glimpse of his beloved Valley

FISHER'S GAP AND FRANKLIN CLIFFS

Hotchkiss wrote that on Tuesday, November 25 "the General crossed the Blue Ridge by Risher's [Fisher's], or Graves' Gap, through Criglersville to Madison C.H. and to a half mile beyond, on the road to Gordonsville."

At one point, probably near Franklin Cliffs, on his crossing of the gap, Private John H. Worsham of the 21st Virginia Infantry wrote:

> Near the top, as we were marching, there was a rock, and looking back and down the road, we could see six lines of our army; in one place infantry, in another artillery, in another ambulances and wagons. Some seemed to be coming towards us, some going to the right, some to the left, and some going away from us. They were all, however, climbing the winding mountain road, and following us.

Jackson is said to have spent a short time at Franklin Cliffs watching his troops climb the winding road and taking a last glimpse of the Valley.

View of the Site of the Village of Mauck (From the author's collection)

To **Stop No. 49**, Continue along this road. At .3 miles it becomes Kite Hollow Road. After another .1 miles; turn right on Red Gate Road. Be very careful as this is a winding, gravel road. After approximately .4 miles you will come to a dead end at Red Gate Road in the Shenandoah National Park. Private vehicles are not permitted on Red Gate Road. For those that wish to see Fishers Gap and Franklin Cliffs, where Jackson took his last glimpse of the Valley. Skyline Drive can be reached along Rt. 211 east of Luray or on Rt. 33 east of Elkton.

View from atop the Skyline
Drive, looking west from
Fisher's Gap (From the
author's collection)

Gen. Stonewall Jackson. The
last photo of General Jackson
prior to his wounding and
subsequent death on May 10,
1863. (National Archives)

View from Franklin Cliffs from where Jackson was said to have taken his last look upon the Shenandoah Valley

TOUR 8

February–December 1863
The Passing of Armies

Begin **Tour No. 8** at **Stop No. 50** at the intersection of Nauman Lane and Honeyville Road/Rt. 638. The tour is approximately 19.6 miles in length and includes 5 stops at historic buildings and sites and ends in Luray. Refer to the maps on pages 107, 110, and 111 for assistance in locating the sites on this tour.

Above: An early view of the old Stoneberger Church between Honeyville and Marksville (From *Page: County of Plenty*)

Brothers Divided

SITE OF STONEBERGER CHURCH

THOUGH NO LONGER STANDING, THE STONEBERGER Church was located just to the east near Stony Run Creek. According to Nauman family stories, at the opening of the Civil War, three of John Perry and Lucy Anne Petefish Nauman's sons left home to serve in the war. While twenty-two-year-old Robert Franklin Nauman chose to serve with Co. K, 10th Virginia Infantry, his eighteen-year-old brother, William D. Nauman, enlisted in the Dixie Artillery. However, twenty-year-old Thomas Jefferson Nauman apparently opted for the Union army. The rift the split-decision must have caused can only be speculated upon as no family record was left that discusses it. However, years after the war descendants of Thomas' siblings recollected that the Union Nauman had been bold enough to return home during a furlough.

On February 17, 1863, while in the schoolyard of the Stoneberger Church, Thomas came up against Lt. Oliver Hazard Perry Kite of Co. H, 33rd Virginia Infantry, and a "mulatto by the name of Richardson." Lieutenant Kite had been home for less than two weeks with about ten men from the company on detail to catch deserters. Richardson shot and killed Thomas Nauman. One source states that children were in the school at the time and saw it happen, but were rushed back into the school and were not allowed out for sometime.

In less than three months, Thomas' brother William was killed while serving with the Purcell Artillery, to which he had transferred, at the Battle of Chancellorsville on May 2. The oldest brother, Robert Franklin, was captured at Gettysburg only two months after William's death. He followed the other two brothers in death while held as a prisoner of war at Ft. Delaware, Delaware.

The Carolina Cavalrymen

GRAVES' CHAPEL MARKER

In March 1863 as elements of Gen. Wade Hampton's old legion passed through the area, the church was turned into a makeshift hospital.

Believed to be either from North or South Carolina, the Unknown Confederate did not die in the church but was said to have expired under a blanket of snow overnight in a field nearby. A "man of medium build and a blond, who evidently went to sleep on his leafy bed without complaining of any ills but died about 3 A.M." The following morning at "about 10 A.M. the regiment had moved on, but two of his cousins had been detailed to give the body proper burial." Samuel M. Larkins prepared a poplar coffin, stained red and jack-planed to create a finish. For a soldier, it was believed that "he was buried as well, or possibly a little better than most of the soldier dead." For his work, Larkin was given $5.

The second Carolinian, William F. Bruner, was of the Wassamassaw Cavalry of Co. D, 2nd South Carolina Cavalry. A dark complexioned man with a jet-black beard, Bruner, was suffering from some ailment and had been

Stop No. 46a is approximately 2.1 away on Chapel Road/ Rt. 611. Some content on the Virginia Civil War Trails marker discusses the two Carolinians buried nearby.

Because of two late nineteenth/early twentieth-century articles in the local newspapers and one in an issue of Confederate Veteran Magazine, *the two graves of Carolina Confederates were finally marked by the local Summers–Koontz Camp No. 490, Sons of Confederate Veterans, in this cemetery in November 2001.*

Graves' Chapel Cemetery. In addition to the Confederate Carolinians, several local Confederate Veterans are also buried in the Graves' Chapel Cemetery. (From the author's collection)

brought into Graves' Chapel where he died in the church 'hospital,' on "two of the short benches; used in the so-called amen corner. He was buried beside the first man and in the same manner, and also by Mr. Larkins."

Grave of Pvt. William F. Bruner, Graves' Chapel Cemetery. Note the pointed top of this and other Confederate stones manufactured by the Veterans Administration. The belief is that Confederates wanted this trait to distinguish their stones from those of the Union soldiers and was to deter "Yankees from sitting on the stones." (From the author's collection)

Unknown Confederate Soldier. Believed to have been a sergeant with the surname of either Litterberry or Whistleberry, this soldier, unlike Private Bruner, cannot be matched to an existing record of a named Confederate soldier, leaving this soldier as an unknown. (From the author's collection)

Stop No. 51 is approximately 7.35 miles away along Deford Street in Luray.

Stop No. 52 is approximately 4.75 miles away on Red Church Road, just off Rt. 211 West. You will first need to get on Rt. 211 East. There will be an opportunity to crossover to Rt. 211 West along the way. Turn right on Red Church Road. A Virginia Civil War Trails marker is in the field immediately to the front of the church.

Silent Reminder of the Retreat from Gettysburg

GEORGE W. HARDIE GRAVE

Though yet unmarked, this private cemetery contains the remains of Ensign (color/standard bearer) George W. Hardie of the 2nd Battalion Georgia Infantry. He was likely brought here as a casualty with most of the Second Corps, Army of Northern Virginia on the retreat from Gettysburg and Manassas Gap (Wapping Heights). He is believed to have died in the Flinn House to the right of the family cemetery.

Page Witnesses the Retreat from Gettysburg

PASS RUN/BETHLEHEM LUTHERAN CHURCH

Nearly three weeks after the Battle of Gettysburg and in the wake of a sharp fight near Front Royal at Wapping Heights (Manassas Gap) on July 23, 1863, Confederate troops from Gen. Richard S. Ewell's corps withdrew to the Page Valley. On July 25 Gen. Robert E. Rodes' division

Eastbound view along the old New Market to Sperryville Turnpike toward Thornton Gap, circa 1910 (Shenandoah Publishing House Post Card, from the author's collection)

camped near Bethlehem Lutheran Church (otherwise known as Red or Brick Church) and along Pass Run. Gen. Edward "Allegheny" Johnson's division camped near Rodes, while Gen. Jubal A. Early's division spent the night at Mt. Jackson.

The soldiers rested the following day, a Sunday, and many attended the Rev. Beverly Tucker Lacy's sermon at headquarters that morning. Before Stonewall Jackson's death near Chancellorsville that spring, Lacy had been his "field minister."

Later that evening, the army began to move again, and Early's division marched through the Massanutten/Luray/New Market Gap into the Page Valley to join the balance of Ewell's Corps.

On the morning of July 27, leaving several of the wounded from Gettysburg and Wapping Heights in Luray in the care of private citizens, Rodes' and Johnson's divisions crossed Thornton Gap into Rappahannock County; Early soon joined them. In the weeks that followed, during what became known as the Bristoe Campaign, both armies fought a series of engagements well into October.

Stop No. 53 is approximately 5.4 miles away along S. Court Street in Luray. This area is one of two possible sites for the original location of the Borst Tannery. The other possible site is near the northwest intersection of the New Market to Sperryville and Luray to Front Royal Turnpikes.

A December Raid on Luray

Borst's Tannery Site

Searching for Gen. Thomas L. Rosser's Confederate cavalry on December 22, Col. Charles H. Smith, commanding the 2nd, 8th, and 16th Pennsylvania Cavalry, and the 2nd Maine Cavalry, entered the Page Valley along the New Market to Sperryville Turnpike through Thornton Gap. Though meeting nominal resistance by a few guerrillas from Maj. Harry Gilmor's command, Smith's party reached a point just four miles from Luray that night.

On the following morning, with the 2nd Pennsylvania as a vanguard, the Federal expedition continued and was met by another "small picket force" that was "easily brushed away." When within sight of Luray, the Federals again encountered yet a third group of about thirty men who were charged and driven through the town with a loss of at least two prisoners, and by evening, two deserters.

Learning that Rosser had been in the town only two days before, Smith began to order detachments to investigate the town. After examining a number of public build-

Union Col. Charles H. Smith
(From *Photographic History of the Civil War: Vol. 10, Armies and Leaders*)

Confederate Gen. Thomas Lafayette Rosser
(*Photographic History of the Civil War: Vol. IV, The Cavalry*)

ings, it was ascertained that "some conscripts had been removed on the news of our approach." Of greater interest however was the "three-story building (Borst's tannery) used as an extensive manufactory of Confederate bridles, saddles, artillery harness, and etc.," that were "well filled with leather, buckles, rings, tools, and everything requisite for such an establishment, together with a large supply of articles ready manufactured." Next to the large building was the tannery "with vats filled with stock, and storehouses full of leather and raw material." Smith wasted no time in denying the resources to future Confederate operations and put the buildings to the torch. In addition to Borst's tannery, the Federals had also destroyed Britton's shops and broke up Gilmor's camp equipage.

Smith soon after withdrew from Luray over concerns that his brigade may be exposed to an attack by a larger Confederate force.

Borst's tannery had not seen the end of the Federal torch. On October 6, 1864, amidst the period known as the "Burning," the establishment was again laid to waste with a loss of over $800,000 in leather goods.

TOUR 9

May 1864
New Market

Begin **Tour No. 9** at New Market/ Massanutten Gap **(Stop No. 33b)** on Rt. 211 on the Page/Shenandoah County line. This is a one-stop tour, unless you proceed on to New Market Battlefield, which can be reached after approximately 5 miles. Refer to the map on page 110 for assistance in locating this site.

Union Gen. David McMurtrie Gregg. (From *Generals in Blue*)

The extremely nice Hall of Valor Museum and New Market Battlefield is a short 5 mile drive from this point to the west, just off of Old Cross Road/Rt. 211 West in New Market.

Conscription and Prelude to New Market

THE THIRD YEAR OF WAR CAME IN WITH A VERY DIFFERENT sense of war than what had existed in the two previous years in the Page Valley. By 1864 the Confederacy had expanded the age-range of those eligible for military service. Though conscription had already been taking place earlier in the war, in 1864 it became a critical matter in sustaining the war effort. On February 28 Union Gen. David McM. Gregg, of the 2nd Cavalry Division, was to enter Page County and "collect the families about Luray that wish to come within our lines to escape the effects of conscription."

While there is no clear record of what happened when Gregg came into Luray, or if he actually did so, Page County did see the creation of several reserve companies throughout 1864. Among these were included Capt. Thomas Keyser's Boy Company (consisting of boys between the ages of seventeen and eighteen) and the 8th Battalion Virginia Reserves.

Even though reserve units had been created, by mid-April conscription (drafting) had apparently escalated a great deal. Records indicate that a number of conscripts may have been generated from Captain Keyser's Boy Company. A fair number of young and older Page County men were assigned to Capt. T. M. Grigsby's Company (later 2nd Co. M), of Col. George H. Smith's 62nd Virginia Infantry on May 4 and were in battle at New Market by May 15.

Boyd's Folly

NEW MARKET/MASSANUTTEN GAP

On May 11 Union Gen. Franz Sigel was in Woodstock with his eyes toward New Market. With interest in the fair amount of Confederate activity in Page County on his eastern flank and the cloaked approach to New Market, Sigel dispatched Col. William H. Boyd with a 300-man detachment of cavalry to scout east through the Blue Ridge Mountains and then approach the village of New Market from the direction of Luray. Unbeknownst to Boyd,

Confederate Gen. John D. Imboden's had arrived in New Market on May 12.

By late in the day on Friday, May 13, Boyd, having kept his movements discrete, had arrived at New Market Gap, having marched through Ashby's Gap to east of the Blue Ridge, reentered the Valley, and made his way through Luray where he destroyed a considerable amount of Confederate commissary supplies. Imboden had given a report only the day before that he had occupied Luray with an outpost under the command of Capt. Harrison H. Riddleberger.

As Boyd pressed on toward New Market, his men spotted troops in the field about the town. To perhaps nearly everyone in Boyd's command, excepting Boyd himself, it was believed that the troops near New Market were Confederates. Just as the lead of the Federal column had made their way across the bridge at Smith Creek, the Confederates under Imboden struck Boyd's detachment. The result of the affair led to the total route of Boyd's troopers, who did not find their way back to Sigel's command for days. Though a small engagement, the encouraging results of the action seemed to heighten the spirits of the Confederates at New Market and set the stage for the battle that followed two days later.

Confederate Capt. Harrison Holt Riddleberger of the 18th Virginia Cavalry was a native of Edinburg, Shenandoah County. Shortly after his duties in Luray in the spring of 1864 he was captured and spent the remainder of the war as a POW. He later served as a U.S. Senator from 1883 to 1889. *(Biographical Directory of the United States Congress)*

Confederate Gen. John D. Imboden
(From Generals in Gray)

Begin **Tour No. 10** at Overall/Milford **(Stop No. 43a)** along Rt. 340 on the Page/Warren County line. You will likely find a better opportunity to pull-off somewhere along Rt. 340 North of the county line and read the description of the opening of Torbert's advance and the action at Milford. The 2-stop tour between Overall and Luray is approximately 11.5 miles in length. Refer to the maps on pages 107 and 110 for assistance in locating the sites on this tour.

Confederate Col. Thomas T. Munford (Library of Congress)

Fishers Hill and Early's Endangered Right

SEPTEMBER 22 – 25, 1864

IN THE AFTERMATH OF A DEVASTATING DEFEAT AT THE Battle of Opequon/Third Winchester, Confederate forces in the area were forced to retreat to Fishers Hill and prepare for another attack from Union forces under Gen. Philip H. Sheridan. Within two days, Sheridan was moving against Early again in what he planned to be the end of Confederate resistance in the Valley.

Sheridan quickly dispatched Gen. Alfred T. A. Torbert to take Col. Wesley Merritt's 1st Division and join Col. James H. Wilson's 3rd Division at Front Royal. From there, the combined Federal cavalry arm would move along the eastern side of the Massanutten through the Page Valley. The intent was that while Sheridan struck hard against Early's left flank with the bulk of his force, Torbert would cross the New Market Gap and surprise Early on the right.

Anticipating such a maneuver, Early had sent Fitz Lee's Division of cavalry, under Williams C. Wickham, up the Luray Valley. Clashing first with the Federals at Riverton on the Shenandoah River, then later on Gooney Run in Warren County on September 21, Wickham temporarily stalled Torbert's efforts.

"Johnnys in a Strong Position"

MILFORD FIGHT (OVERALL)

Merritt's and Wilson's divisions closed on Milford on September 22 and found Wickham's position along Overall Run a challenge to overcome. A Michigander serving with George A. Custer, in Merritt's division, wrote in his diary, "Johnnys in a strong position."

Nonetheless, Wilson opened the action with artillery, which was soon joined by the crackle of Federal carbine fire. The Confederate forces soon responded in kind. While the rolling terrain rocked with a "ringing fire," Wickham rode off to consult with Early over the situation, leaving Col. Thomas T. Munford to conduct the defense.

The fire continued for hours with little progress made by Torbert. However, late in the afternoon he appeared to move against Col. William Payne's brigade along the river.

Witnessing the effort, Munford asked his artillery commander, Maj. James Breathed, if he thought his guns were safe from capture. In response, Breathed proclaimed, "If 'Billy' [Payne] can hold that bridge—and it looks like he is going to do it—I'll put a pile of cannister [sic] near my guns, and all hell will never move me from this position."

Meanwhile, Munford realized the movement on Payne was a feinted attack, designed to distract from an effort to turn his right flank. In response, Munford sent a squadron of the 4th Virginia Cavalry to the support of the 2nd Virginia on his right. Additionally three buglers were sent to create a bluff. When given the order, the buglers, spaced at good intervals, sounded the charge and forced the Federals to abandon the maneuver.

Disgruntled, Torbert broke off the engagement and withdrew toward Front Royal. However, by late in the afternoon of September 23 Torbert received word from Sheridan that he had won at Fisher's Hill and desired him to "push down the Luray Valley without regard to horseflesh." Finding the position previously held by the Confederates abandoned, Torbert bivouacked for the night near Milford. Torbert resumed the advance on September 24, with Merritt in the lead.

Union Gen. Alfred T. A. Torbert
(From *Generals in Blue*)

Custer's Charge and the collapse of Confederate Cavalry at Luray

YAGER'S MILL MARKER

As Merritt closed in on Luray, Payne's Confederate brigade, ordered to return to Milford and unaware of Merritt's progress beyond Springfield, came into contact here with Merritt's troopers.

Payne quickly dismounted the 5th and 6th Virginia Cavalry and placed them on the right behind fence rails along the Luray Road, while the 15th Virginia Cavalry was held mounted to the left of the road near Yager's Mill and "concealed by a small skirt of woods and a high fence." As the Federals moved in, they brought their artillery into battery atop a height overlooking the Confederate position and began to open up. Shortly thereafter, Gen. George A. Custer, leading the 6th Michigan and two squadrons of the 2nd Massachusetts, descended from the Federal left while the 1st Michigan thundered down the main road. A

Confederate Maj. James Breathed
(*The Long Arm of Lee*, vol. II)

For **Stop No. 54**, from Overall, follow Rt. 340 South to Luray for approximately 11.5 miles and turn right at the Park and Ride near town. Once you turn in, you will see a Virginia Civil War Trails marker near the foot bridge to your left.

Nº 25.

SKETCH

OF THE

CAVALRY ENGAGEMENT

AT

MILFORD, VA.,

OF

FITZ LEE'S DIVISION.

Wednesday, Sept. 21st, 1864.

to accompany Report of

JED. HOTCHKISS, Top. Eng. V.D.

Scale : 2 Inches to 1 Mile.

0   1/8   1/4   1/2   3/4   1 Mile.

Top. Eng. Office, V.D., Feb. 22, 1865,
Copied by S. B. Robinson.

RIVER

SHENANDOAH

Leathe's Ford

Milford

△ 12 M.

Fog

PAYNE'S

WICKHAM'S

△ 13 M.

4th Va.

1st Va.

2d Va.

Skirm

JOHNSTON'S Batt'y

FITZ LEE'S DI

2 Squa

School House

14 M. Post from Front Royal.

To Luray

Accompanying the report of Capt. Jed. Hotchkiss, C.S. Army
Top. Engr. 2º Corps, A. of N. Va. (Valley Dist.)
SERIES I. VOL. XLIII. PART 1. PAGE 1027.

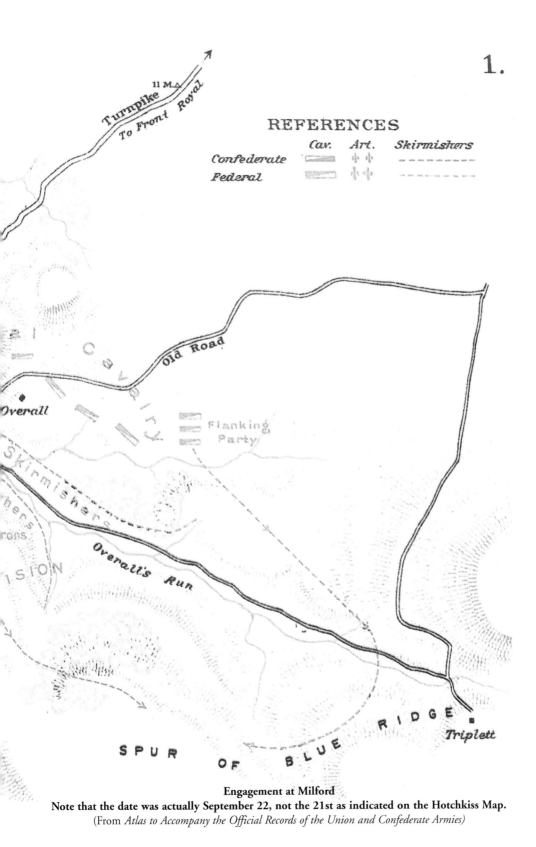

Engagement at Milford
Note that the date was actually September 22, not the 21st as indicated on the Hotchkiss Map.
(From *Atlas to Accompany the Official Records of the Union and Confederate Armies*)

Pvt. Baybutt's Medal of Honor
This is the actual medal earned by English-born Pvt. Philip Baybutt for taking the flag of the 6th Virginia Cavalry in action at Yager's Mill. Baybutt returned to England after the war and despite his having earned the high honor and sustaining injuries in other actions in the war, was refused a veteran's pension from the United States. (Courtesy of Peter Baybutt)

mounted squadron of the 6th Virginia was ordered to countercharge but was quickly overcome by blue troopers to their left and rear. Realizing the severity of the situation many of the Confederate officers then began to tell their men to save themselves.

In less than a half hour, the Federal advance at Yager's Mill had pushed the Confederates toward New Market Gap, with several men taking to the old Luray to Staunton Turnpike (Leaksville Road) and Blue Ridge Turnpike toward Honeyville. There, Payne's men rallied and prepared for another attack by the Federals which did not come.

In all, Torbert reported that his men had captured seventy-two men between Milford and Luray. Also in the affair, Pvt. Philip Baybutt, of Company A, 2nd Massachusetts Cavalry, seized the regimental colors of the 6th Virginia Cavalry, for which he earned a Medal of Honor.

Though he had finally made his way across the Massanutten to New Market by September 25, it was far too late. Wickham had successfully held the line and effectively prevented what could have been the absolute defeat of Early's army. Furthermore, the effort, having prolonged the presence of Early in the Valley, may have prevented Sheridan's return to Gen. Ulysses S. Grant's forces around Petersburg, and thereby delayed the end of the war. Ultimately, Sheridan reported that Torbert's efforts in Page Valley were an "entire failure."

Confederate Col. William H. F. Payne.
(From *Photographic History of the Civil War, Vol. 10, Armies and Leaders.*)

BY LATE SEPTEMBER 1864 UNION GEN. PHILIP H. Sheridan had soundly defeated Confederate forces under Jubal Early in two separate battles and held most of the Shenandoah Valley. However, Sheridan also realize that in order to make his victories even more powerful, something must be done to sever the resources of the "Breadbasket of the Confederacy" from Gen. Robert E. Lee's Army. While Augusta County had witnessed the commencement of burnings on September 27, and Rockingham began to see the effects of the torch on September 30, Shenandoah and Page Counties were yet to be dealt with.

The torches are lit

PRICE'S AND HUFFMAN'S MILLS

On Sunday, October 2, 1864, Sheridan's Second Cavalry Division, under Col. William H. Powell, splashed across Naked Creek and into Page County to commence the destruction of barns, mills, factories, and standing crops as well as the seizure of livestock. Lying near the old Luray to Staunton Turnpike, Price's Mill was likely the first to be burned to the ground.

Further up Naked Creek stood Ambrose Huffman's Mill. In addition to an up-and-down sawmill, the Huffman site included a grist or chopping mill, and a flouring mill. A son of Ambrose, James Huffman later recalled "we had a good barn, lumber mill, merchandise and chopping mill, store, tan-yard, blacksmith shop, ice house and other farm buildings such as meat house, corn house, loom house, hen house and more than three hundred acres of land in the home tract."

To Federal troopers on the way through the county, the Huffman operation offered an excellent target that Sunday morning. When the cavalrymen arrived, they informed Christiana Huffman that they intended to burn the barns and mills of the Valley. Christiana then replied that they had "come to late to burn the barn. A hand more powerful than yours has taken care of that—it was struck by lightening and burned to the ground two weeks ago." While the Federals contented themselves with the mills and store, others took advantage of "a lot of pies" that Christiana' s daughter had been baking that morning.

TOUR 11

October 1864
The Burning

Begin **Tour No. 11** at the site of Price's Mill along Naked Creek, near the Page/Rockingham County line (**Stop No. 41a**). The tour is approximately 32 miles in length and includes 11 stops at historic buildings and sites and ends at Aventine Hill in Luray. Refer to the maps on pages 107, 110, and 111 for assistance in locating the sites on this tour.

Union Col. William H. Powell
(National Archives)

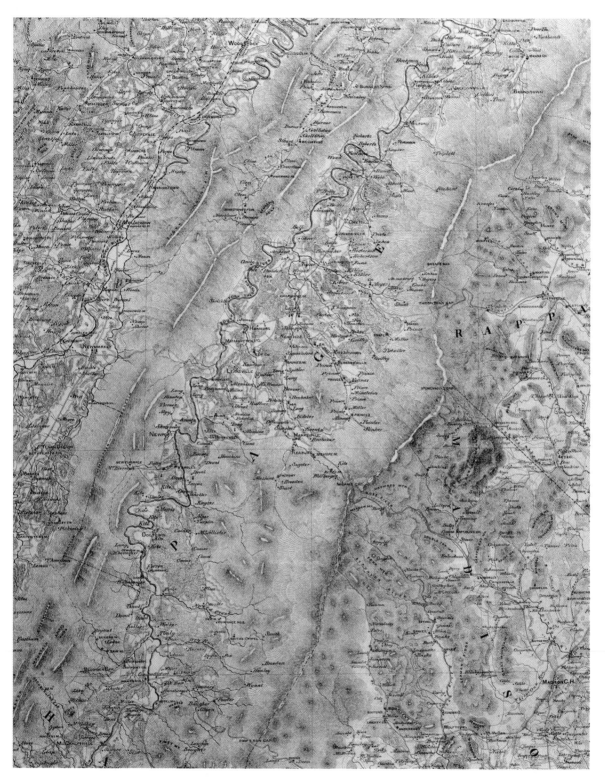

Gilmer Map of Page County in 1864
(Virginia Historical Society,
Richmond, Virginia)

Facing page:
Map of Page County (1862) by Jedediah Hotchkiss
(Library of Congress)

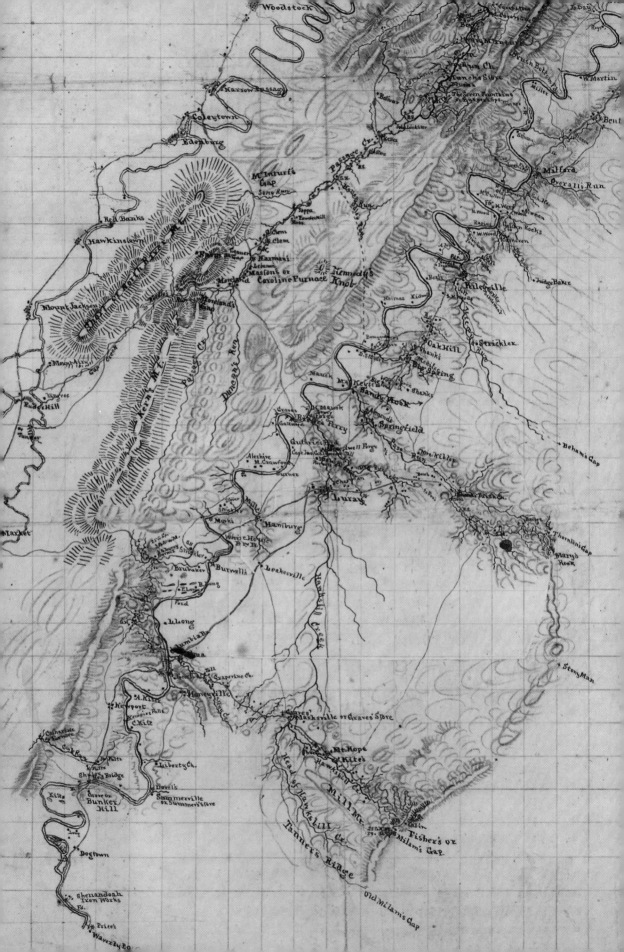

Price's Mill. Like the one on Tour 5, this view is postwar; the original mill likely being the first burned in Page County after Powell's arrival in October 1864.
(From *Shenandoah: A History of Our Town and Its People*)

Stop No. 40a is approximately 11 miles away at the Alma boat landing off of River Road/Rt. 650.

Patrols fan out across the county

SITE OF NOAH KITE'S "COLUMBIA MILL"

The Federal cavalry pressed on toward Luray, leaving a line of devastation in their wake. When they reached Noah Kite's Mill, "full of grain and feed," it too received the torch. It was from this point near Alma that the cavalry broke up into detachments. One would move along the river; another took toward Mill Creek and yet a third raced off to the Little Hawksbill and then on to Hawksbill proper.

Eggs for a barn

BURNER HOUSE—"MASSANUTTEN HEIGHTS"
National Register of Historic Places

From "Massanutten Heights," the Burner family could easily see plumes of smoke from the distant mills already set ablaze. John A. Burner, the head of the family, hurriedly gathered his cattle and placed them in a ravine behind the house. Apparently, the first of the Federals to pass included men of the 2nd Pennsylvania Cavalry, driving quite a herd of captured cattle past the farm. Burner's cows could not resist but follow the clanking of bells and lowing of other cattle as they passed and soon moved along to join the drove. All efforts by Burner to turn them back failed.

Thoroughly disheartened by the loss of his livestock, Burner sat down on his porch and began to sing hymns aloud. No sooner had he begun the soothing remedy, than two Federal cavalrymen arrived and proclaimed, "We've come to burn your barn!" Burner stopped singing, pointed to the barn and said, "There it is. Burn it." Spurring their horses on to the structure, Burner's boys, Danny (9), Isaac

Stop No. 34a is approximately 4.5 miles away off of Rt. 211.

Wheat fields near Luray, circa 1910. The Shenandoah Valley had a high yield in grains in 1864, setting the stage for immense losses from the Burning. The Federal troops finally moved out of the Page Valley after almost a week, on Friday, October 7. Historian Harry M. Strickler estimated a loss of 300 barns and over $600,000 in property in Page County as a result of Powell's efforts. On October 24, 1864, the county appealed to the Confederate government for relief from the conscription of so many men in order to return to the farms for fear of starvation among the civilian population. (Courtesy of the Ann Vaughn Collection)

Map of Shenandoah Iron Works (July 1865) by Jedediah Hotchkiss
(Library of Congress)

Facing page:
Contemporary map of Civil War sites in Luray
(Created by Bil Cullen, Communication Design)

Avenue of Armies
Luray Sites

1. The Peter B. Borst House "Aventine"
2. The Benjamin F. Grayson House "Cottage on the Cliff"
3. The Page County Court House
4. The Frank & Cornelia Jordan House "Cliff Cottage"
5. The Mann Spitler House "Hotel Laurence"
6. The Nicholas W. Yager House
7. The Gabriel Jordan House "Mansion Inn"
8. The Macon Jordan House
9. The John Lionberger House
13. The William A. Chapman/ Ruffner House
14. The Samuel Moore House
27. Aventine Hill (Mimslyn)
31. Cave Hill (Luray Caverns)
32. Luray to Staunton Turnpike
37. Luray Road (Old Luray to Front Royal Turnpike)
42. Augustus S. Modesitt Residence
44. Cavalry Engagement Marker
51. Ensign George W. Hardie Grave, Flinn Yard
53. Borst's Tannery Site
54. Yager's Mill Marker
59. Willow Grove Mill
66. Green Hill Cemetery
67. Barbee Confederate Monument
68. 1918 Confederate Veterans Monument
69. Luray Train Depot
70. Inn Lawn Park
A. New Market to Sperryville Turnpike

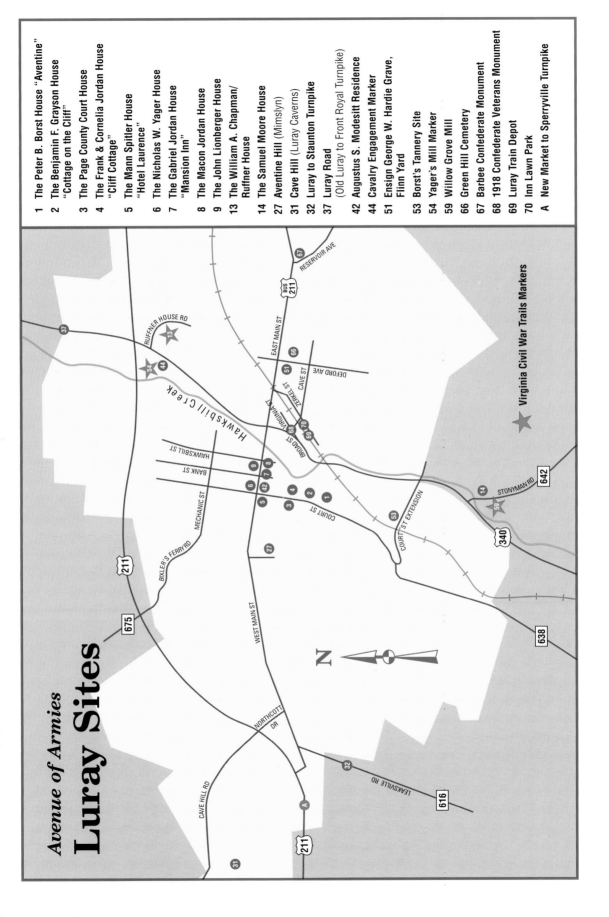

This circa 1910 glimpse of the area below Canada's Peak reveals an area that glowed red with the fires from barns and mills on the night of October 2, 1864. (D. L. Kauffman Post Card, from the author's collection)

(7) and Davy (6) hurried behind the troopers. Three weeks short of his tenth birthday, Danny spoke out to the men before they laid the barn to waste, "Let me get the eggs" and ran into the barn, bringing out four or five-dozen. In turn, the boy must have struck a soft spot with the senior cavalryman present, when he stated to the boy, "Captain, I'll take your eggs and leave your barn." Realizing the immense bargain, the boy smiled as he handed the eggs to the Federal. Later, when the father asked why the barn had not been burned, Danny responded, "We traded. They took the eggs and left me the barn."

Godly intervention

MARTIN STRICKLER SITE

Prior to reaching "Massanutten Heights," Federal cavalrymen arrived here in Leaksville soon after being divided into detachments at Columbia Mill. A short distance north of this stop, Peggy Kite Strickler looked to the east and south and saw "many barns blazing." Though there is no mention of her husband at the time of the burning, Martin, a former Confederate officer, may have rounded the family livestock or other goods and headed to the mountains once

Stop No. 55 is approximately 4.3 miles away at the intersection of Ganders Drive and Leaksville Road/Rt. 616.

the approach of Federals had been learned. Nevertheless, to help with the household, Martin's sister, Mary Catherine, had come to live with the family before Martin's departure to war.

When the Federals arrived and began laying torches on the outbuildings and barn, Catherine ran to the barn and called to the soldiers to stop. Paying no attention to her pleas, Catherine looked to heaven and raised her arms in an effort to invoke the help of God. According to family legend, clouds rolled over the farm and a brief torrent quickly put out the fires. Hurrying to the Strickler kitchen, the cavalrymen re-ignited their brands and set the barn afire again. Still, Catherine sought a higher power and again a rain passed to put out the fire. After yet a third attempt and yet another brief downpour, the frustrated Federals departed, leaving only a partially scorched structure.

The firewitch

Martin Coffman Site

When cavalrymen arrived at the nearby farm of forty-nine-year-old Martin D. Coffman, the Federals were in for yet another supernatural surprise. Martin was one of those who, many believed, had been blessed by special powers, a "fire witch" as some said. The belief was not at all uncommon with the old world Germanic beliefs that had been passed through the generations. When a cavalryman entered Coffman's barn and began to kindle a blaze, the farmer followed and placed his hand on the Federal's shoulder. At once the small blaze went out. Again the soldier tended to his chore and again Coffman, with the same practice, seemed to put an end to it. Unholstering his revolver, the cavalryman ordered Coffman out of the barn, to which he replied, "I can't stop you from doing this, but you are going to a bad end." As he walked out, he turned again to the trooper and proclaimed, "I could cause you to burst into flames." Though he did not demonstrate the threat, the thought must have lingered on the trooper's mind as the barn eventually went up in flames. According to legend, the Federals were the same group of men from the 6th Ohio Cavalry that met a deadly fate on the Hershberger Farm near Luray.

Stop No. 56 is approximately 1 mile away along Mt. Carmel Rd./Rt. 629.

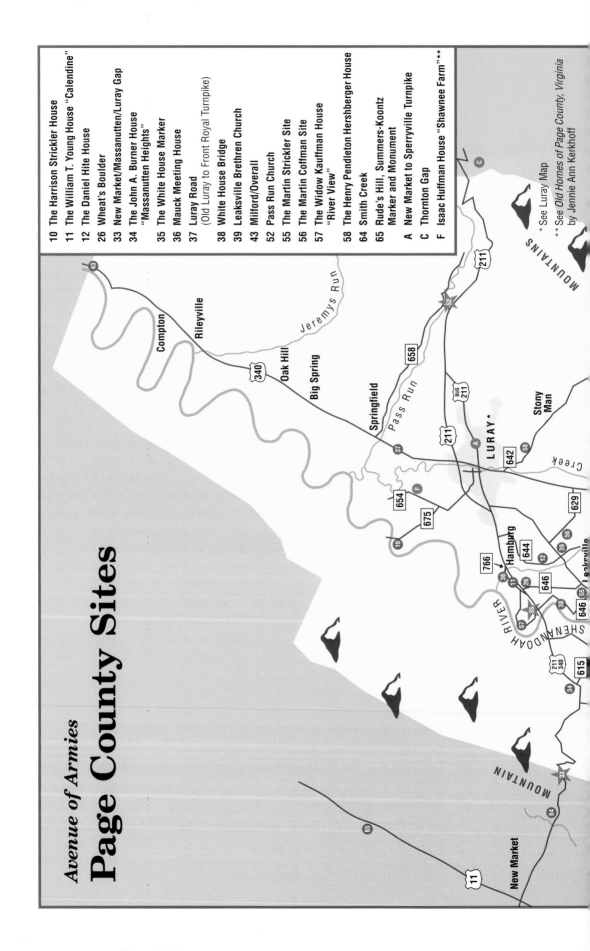

Avenue of Armies
Page County Sites

10 The Harrison Strickler House
11 The William T. Young House "Calendine"
12 The Daniel Hite House
26 Wheat's Boulder
33 New Market/Massanutten/Luray Gap
34 The John A. Burner House
     "Massanutten Heights"
35 The White House Marker
36 Mauck Meeting House
37 Luray Road
     (Old Luray to Front Royal Turnpike)
38 White House Bridge
39 Leaksville Brethren Church
43 Milford/Overall
52 Pass Run Church
55 The Martin Strickler Site
56 The Martin Coffman Site
57 The Widow Kauffman House
     "River View"
58 The Henry Pendleton Hershberger House
64 Smith Creek
65 Rude's Hill, Summers-Koontz
     Marker and Monument
A New Market to Sperryville Turnpike
C Thornton Gap
F Isaac Huffman House "Shawnee Farm"***

 * See Luray Map
** See *Old Homes of Page County, Virginia*
     by Jennie Ann Kerkhoff

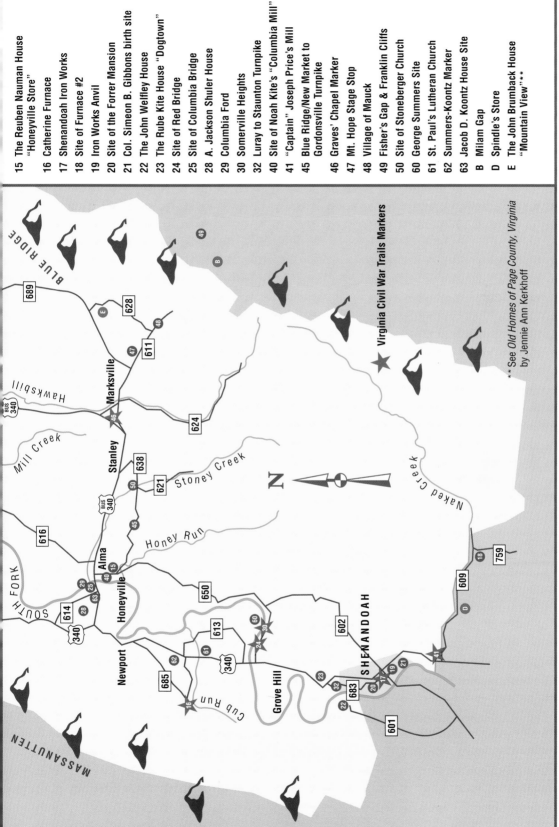

15 The Reuben Nauman House
   "Honeyville Store"
16 Catherine Furnace
17 Shenandoah Iron Works
18 Site of Furnace #2
19 Iron Works Anvil
20 Site of the Forrer Mansion
21 Col. Simeon B. Gibbons birth site
22 The John Welfley House
23 The Rube Kite House "Dogtown"
24 Site of Red Bridge
25 Site of Columbia Bridge
28 A. Jackson Shuler House
29 Columbia Ford
30 Somerville Heights
32 Luray to Staunton Turnpike
40 Site of Noah Kite's "Columbia Mill"
41 "Captain" Joseph Price's Mill
45 Blue Ridge/New Market to
   Gordonsville Turnpike
46 Graves' Chapel Marker
47 Mt. Hope Stage Stop
48 Village of Mauck
49 Fisher's Gap & Franklin Cliffs
50 Site of Stoneberger Church
60 George Summers Site
61 St. Paul's Lutheran Church
62 Summers-Koontz Marker
63 Jacob D. Koontz House Site
B Milam Gap
D Spindle's Store
E The John Brumback House
   "Mountain View"**

Virginia Civil War Trails Markers

** See *Old Homes of Page County, Virginia*
   by Jennie Ann Kerkhoff

Contemporary map of Civil War Sites in Page County (Created by Bil Cullen, Communication Design)

The Widow Kauffman House, "Riverview" (From the author's collection)

Stop No. 57 is approximately 4 miles away along Kauffman's Mill Road/Rt. 646.

The Capture of the Kauffman Brothers

WIDOW KAUFFMAN HOUSE "RIVER VIEW"

Built around 1820, at the time of the war "River View" was home to the widow Rebecca Kauffman. Three of her sons fell-in with over 1,000 other men from Page that served during the war. Her eldest, Joseph Franklin Kauffman, lay in the family cemetery nearby, killed at the Battle of 2nd Manassas in the summer of 1862.

By the time of the arrival of Powell's Federals in October, son Enoch V. Kauffman, a twenty-four-year-old sergeant of the 10th Virginia Infantry happened to be home. Caught in the stampede route from the battle of Fisher's Hill, he had taken temporary refuge in the mountains and had arrived at home by the end of September. Coincidentally, seventeen-year-old Philip M. Kauffman, a private with Company E, 35th Battalion Virginia Cavalry, was also visiting home at the same time, having been assigned to a scouting detail in the area.

Once a Federal burning party had seen to the destruction of the Joel Mauck Mill immediately across the road from the Kauffman House, they had been informed that the Kauffman brothers were hiding around the house.

A search commenced for the two Confederates, who were later found. Despite the pleas and weeping of Rebecca, the men were taken to Luray, near Col. Powell's headquarters on the knoll on the western edge of town. There they were locked up and held under guard until the colonel could find time to deal with them.

The stern decision of Col. Powell

AVENTINE HILL

In the days following October 2, Powell sent out detachments from his headquarters near here on various missions to protect Sheridan's flank. One detail headed for the Blue Ridge and was informed by Northern sympathizers of a band of bushwhackers at a certain location. The Federals subsequently attacked and killed at least one man before destroying the camp. Powell reported that his men had surprised a party of bushwhackers, destroyed their rendezvous, capturing two prisoners, 10 wagons (loaded with plunder of every description), medical supplies to the value of $5,000, horses, mules, etc and sent one bushwhacker to his long home." As that detail was headed back to Luray,

Site of the Joel Mauck Mill and "Old Fredericksburg"
(From the author's collection)

Stop No. 27b is approximately 3.5 miles away along Main Street in Luray, in front of the Mimslyn.

113

one Federal cavalryman was found with his throat cut. At once Powell flew into a rage and, by October 3, ordered the Kauffmans, captured the day before, to be executed in retaliation. At about the same time, Rebecca Kauffman and a daughter had come to Luray asking about her sons. Hearing of their pronounced fate, Rebecca gained an audience with Powell but was told nothing could be done for them. With no hope, the widowed mother left in tears from the colonel's headquarters.

The death of two mountain boys

PETER B. BORST'S AVENTINE

Stop No. 1a is approximately .3 miles away along S. Court Street, Luray.

It is believed that upon the return of the patrols from the Blue Ridge, Federals brought in with them "two mountain boys," aged eleven and thirteen, who had been shot. Bringing the boys to Aventine, the "officers sent word down town, that if any ladies wished, they could come up and attend the boys. According to Mrs. Sue Heiskell, she, along with Sally Lionberger made their way to Aventine to offer what help they could. "We went there and there laid those poor boys stretched out on boards, with blood dripping from them," recalled Mrs. Heiskell.

> The Yankees refused to have a doctor attend them, and gave us no medicine or anything to work with. They were so pale. I cared for one and Sally the other. One kept saying, 'I want my mother, I want my mother,' until he was too weak to say it aloud, but I could see him say it in his mind . . . We comforted them as best we could but there was little we could do, as it was too late when we were called.

A pivotal clash of patrols

PENDLETON HERSHBERGER HOUSE

Stop No. 58 is approximately 1.6 miles away along Stonyman Rd./Rt. 642.

Near Stonyman in Page County at the home of Pendleton Hershberger, Elizabeth Beaver Hershberger and several of her children watched in horror as many barns and buildings were torched by the Federal soldiers. Late in the day on October 2, three troopers of the Company F, 6th

Ohio Cavalry came to call and demanded $30 or $40 in gold or else they would burn the barn. Amidst the pleas of the children not to do the deed, the explanation was given that they did not have such money.

Shortly after a band of Confederates rode up the lane and took the Federal horse-holder in the lane. At least two of the party approached the two Federals at the house. Demanding that the Federals surrender, one of the Ohioans

The Henry Pendleton Hershberger House. This circa 1900 photo of the Hershberger House shows the original clapboard appearance. The lane leading to the house was on the right. (Courtesy of E. A. Poe)

Modern view of the Hershberger House (From the author's collection)

115

Circa 1900 view reminiscent of the time of the war
(D. L. Kauffman Postcard, from the author's collection)

Pvt. Arthur Callison was one of the Federal troopers killed in the clash at the Hershberger House incident. Though originally buried on the farm, like many other Federal soldiers buried in Page County, he was relocated after the war to the National Cemetery in Staunton. (Photo by the author)

Stop No. 59 is approximately .9 miles away along Stonyman Rd./Rt. 642.

stepped further up on the porch, "placing himself in front of the family for protection, suddenly turned and with a loud oath said, 'I will surrender you,' at the same time, firing point blank at one of the Confederates, but missed him . . ."

As soon as the first shot had been fired, the Hershberger family was hurried back into the home and "saw no more of the fight." By the end of the shoot-out, at least two Federals lay dead, including Pvt. Arthur Callison.

The next day, as suspected, Union cavalry arrived at the homestead "in a very angry mood." However, the details of the story were already known by the Federals and "did not blame any of the family for anything, except that they had let the man lie there all day in the sun." The result of this action ultimately encouraged, even more, Powell's decision to execute the Kauffman brothers.

Another casualty of Red October

WILLOW GROVE MILL

Pre-dating the existence of the town of Luray, the old village of Mundellsville that stood here was also the site of Willow Grove Mill. By the time of the war, the mill had

been sold several times. In 1864 Samuel Moore was the owner. Though he did not reside here, a daughter did and bore witness to the time that many knew as "Red October" for the glow of fires throughout the Valley. Willow Grove Mill was a fine sturdy mill, built of large logs, supported by a high rock foundation and powered by an eighteen-foot overshot wheel. An up-and-down sawmill was connected with the place as well as orchards and a distillery. Of the fateful October day, Amanda Moore recalled that the once amazing operation was in upheaval. "We had the Mill, Saw Mill, barn + all the stabling, grainery [*sic*], corn crib, and everything burnt . . . [T]he barns were full of wheat and there was a great deal in the Mill."

The Crittenden-Hartigan Incident

AVENTINE HILL

Within a few days of the capture of the Kauffman brothers, two Confederates of Company C, 1st Maryland Cavalry were in the Page Valley on a foraging detail. While obtaining supplies from a farmer somewhere near Luray, a Federal patrol closed in on the farmhouse. The Marylanders attempted to escape, but were caught in a running fight. According to a postwar account, Confederate trooper Churchill Crittenden emptied every load in his pistol and wounded "a Yankee lieutenant very severely" before being taken. Confederate John J. Hartigan accompanied

Stop No. 27c is approximately 1.5 miles away on Main Street in Luray.

117

After the Maryland comrades retrieved the bodies, Private Hartigan was relocated to the Emanual Lutheran Church Cemetery in New Market and Crittenden to Shockoe Hill Cemetery in Richmond. (Photo by the author)

Crittenden in the affair and contributed to the deaths of at least two or three Federal troopers in the melee.

After having found one of his troopers with his throat cut, Powell had issued an edict to local citizens promising the death of two bushwhackers for every one of his men killed in the discharge of his duties. Crittenden and Hartigan would be the example that Powell needed. An article in a 1912 Crittenden family newsletter revealed that after having been brought to Powell, the men were taken through a mock trial and ordered to be executed. Both men were refused pen and paper to draft farewell letters.

The executions were carried out on October 4. "At noon Crittenden and Hartigan were set before a firing party of twenty-five and told to run for their lives. Hartigan ran and fell, pierced by many bullets. Crittenden stood with folded arms, facing his executioners. Again the order to fire was given, but not a trigger was pulled. The Union officer in command then addressed his men saying he would repeat the order once more; they were soldiers and must obey, and should any man fail to respect the command, he should suffer the penalty of death himself for his disobedience."

"During this harangue Crittenden seated himself on a rock, calmly looking at the squad and awaiting his end. Then he rose. "Ready! Aim! Fire!" rang out the third command. A line of leveled rifles greeted him as he rose and faced them. Down dropped twenty-four silent rifles, their owners unwilling to harm the quiet man before them. One alone of the twenty-five pressed a trigger. A single flash, a little smoke, a sharp report, and Churchill Crittenden's life blood flowed for the cause he loved."

Ultimately, because of the deaths of the Marylanders, the lives of the Kauffman brothers were spared. Both were sent to Point Lookout, Maryland, as prisoners of war. Philip was exchanged on March 28, 1865, but Enoch was not released until after taking the oath of allegiance on June 14, 1865.

The body of Private Hartigan was relocated to Lutheran Reformed Church cemetery in New Market. Private Crittenden was removed to Shockoe Hill Cemetery in Richmond.

Over a month after Appomattox and the subsequent but separate disbanding of the famous Laurel Brigade, four veterans of the "Massanutten Rangers" of Company D, 7th Virginia Cavalry, set out from their homes in Page County to receive paroles at Woodstock. Capt. George Washington Summers (22), Sgt. Isaac Newton Koontz (20), his cousin Jacob Daniel Koontz (20), and Andrew Jackson Kite (30) started on their way in the early morning hours of May 22, 1865.

When the group came upon about half-a-dozen stragglers from Co. H, 22nd New York Cavalry, the meeting must have been less than cordial and led to the Page men drawing their revolvers and demanding the surrender of the horses. A lieutenant with the band of Federals "resented" the demand and drew his pistol in response. One of the four Confederates turned his piece toward the gun-wielding lieutenant. The hammers on both weapons came down but failed to discharge. Ultimately, the Rochester Cavalrymen reluctantly consented to surrender.

The four Page County men quickly returned to their homes in the Luray Valley only to be received less than favorably by George Summers, Sr. After the facts of the incident had been ascertained, Captain Summers' father set out to gather a group of some of the most prominent citizens to go to the Federal camp the next day and plead that the rashness of the young men be forgiven.

Arriving at the camp of the 192nd Ohio at Rude's Hill on the next day, the elder Summers recollected that they were "courteously" received by Colonel Francis W. Butterfield, commanding the post. After coming to an agreement and the property being returned, receipts were given to the ex-Confederates and a promise made of no retribution for their actions.

A modern scene from near where the George Summers House once stood
(Photo by the author)

TOUR 12

May–June 1865
The Summers-Koontz Incident

Begin **Tour No. 12** at the George Summers Site (**Stop No. 60**) on Old Farm Road, just off of Strole Farm Road/Rt. 613. The tour is approximately 25 miles in length and includes 7 stops at historic sites and ends at Rude's Hill in Shenandoah County, north of New Market. The George Summers House no longer stands but formerly occupied a spot somewhere in the fields to the right. Refer to the maps on pages 110 and 111 for assistance in locating the sites for this tour.

119

Stop No. 61: From the George Summers Site, gain Strole Farm Road to Rt. 340. St. Paul's Lutheran Church is approximately 2.1 miles distant, along Rt. 340.

St. Paul's Lutheran Church
The original congregation of the Monger Church moved to this church within a year or so after the Summers-Koontz Incident. The congregation once included some of the men from the Summers-Koontz Incident (From the author's collection)

An argument in the church

St. Paul's Lutheran Church

Although the matter appeared to be resolved, trouble again surfaced one Sunday in June at the nearby Monger Church (the original church no longer stands and the congregation later moved to this church). A local Union sympathizer, William Tharp, engaged one of the former Confederates in an argument about the Federal property. The elder Summers recollected that Tharp, "became very much enraged." After one of the young men earlier involved in the stolen horse episode made a comment to Tharp, the Unionist snapped back: "You had better return those horses stolen from the Yankees!" At the conclusion of the verbal confrontation one of the young men (but neither Captain Summers nor Sergeant Koontz) threatened to hit Tharp. Tharp swore he would go to the Federal camp and get revenge for his mistreatment.

It is unclear as to whether or not Tharp carried out his threat. However, in the interim Col. Butterfield had gone on furlough leaving a more stringent Lt. Col. Cyrus Hussey in command of the 192nd Ohio.

According to a modern biographer, Lt. Col. Cyrus Hussey was "a stern and righteous man . . . Hussey was a Quaker before the war." However, "he had lost his pacifism but not his self-righteousness [and] that was probably a dangerous combination when he was occupying territory rather than invading it. He apparently never did have a sense of humor."

Federal cavalry comes to call

GEORGE SUMMERS SITE

On Monday, June 26, Special Order No. 3 was issued by Hussey to Capt. Lycurgus D. Lusk, commanding Company H, 22nd New York Cavalry, to "proceed to Luray Valley at 9 P.M. and there arrest and execute severally and all without delay whatsoever, the followed named men who had been guilty of attacking U.S. troops and stealing horses since the surrender." The four young men were named and underlined several times in red. The order for the execution was in accordance with instructions "from Army and Department Headquarters."

Early on the morning of June 27 the detail reached the home of George Summers and proceeded to encircle them. George Summers was determined to make his escape. However, after some convincing by his father, he allowed himself to be arrested to face what his father expected would be a fair trial.

The elder Summers tried to explain the earlier agreement made with Colonel Butterfield and showed the receipts for the returned items, but Captain Lusk was indignant toward Summers and had no knowledge of the transaction. However, Summers had "breakfast prepared for them and they ate at the same table with my son George." When the party was finished and ready to go, the elder Summers stated his willingness to accompany them back to Rude's Hill and see the officer in charge. Captain Lusk in turn told him it would be best to wait until the following day and possibly procure their release. The elder Summers was satisfied that he would be able to do so, but his son felt uneasy and bid farewell as if he were certain he would die.

Stop No. 60a: While you may remain here and continue reading the additional text for the Summers site and proceed on to stop 62, you also have the option to retrace your steps, 2.1 miles to the George Summers site along Strole Farm Road.

George W. Summers, Sr. The war brought a great deal of grief to Summers. In addition to losing his only son, he also lost a daughter, granddaughter, and son-in-law in 1862. (Courtesy of Jo Ann Schaub)

Summers-Koontz Incident Marker. This historical marker is midway between the homes of Captain Summers and Sergeant Koontz. (From the author's collection)

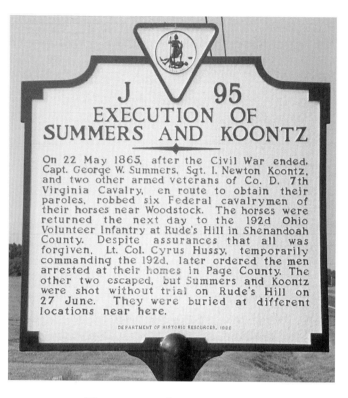

J 95
EXECUTION OF
SUMMERS AND KOONTZ

On 22 May 1865, after the Civil War ended, Capt. George W. Summers, Sgt. I. Newton Koontz, and two other armed veterans of Co. D, 7th Virginia Cavalry, en route to obtain their paroles, robbed six Federal cavalrymen of their horses near Woodstock. The horses were returned the next day to the 192d Ohio Volunteer Infantry at Rude's Hill in Shenandoah County. Despite assurances that all was forgiven, Lt. Col. Cyrus Hussy, temporarily commanding the 192d, later ordered the men arrested at their homes in Page County. The other two escaped, but Summers and Koontz were shot without trial on Rude's Hill on 27 June. They were buried at different locations near here.

DEPARTMENT OF HISTORIC RESOURCES, 1988

The capture of Newton Koontz

THE JACOB DANIEL KOONTZ HOUSE

To **Stop No. 63,** return to Strole Farm Road and continue North for 1.8 miles to Rt. 340. Turn right and proceed for .2 miles. Turn left at the high school to see the Virginia Department of Historic Resources sign **(Stop No. 62)** erected on June 27, 1999 at the edge of the school property along Rt. 340. From there, continue on Rt. 340 North for 2.1 miles. Turn right on Rt. 340 North Business. Continue for 1.2 miles and prior to the cut in the road leading to the bridge, pull-off into the grass-gravel area on the side of the road. Look across the road to see the stone chimney and foundation of the J. D. Koontz House.

Before dawn on June 27 Federal cavalry came to this house and captured Sergeant Koontz. Like Private Kite at his house nearby, Pvt. Jacob D. Koontz was able to get away in time to evade the Federals. Taking Koontz on to Noah Kite's "Columbia Mill," the former sergeant saw a familiar passerby and asked the lieutenant in charge for permission to draft a quick note and have the friend dispatch it to his betrothed, Emma Jane Shuler. The lieutenant agreed and Newton wrote:

> I write to inform you that I was arrested this morning before daylight at Uncle Daniel Koontz's in bed. I am now under arrest . . . I hope dearest Emma you will bear up under this as well as you can, and doubt not but that God will allow me to return to you[.] he will not allow such innocence to be bereft of its happiness. I hope Mr. Shuler will take some interest in my welfare and do some things for me if possible, I expect to be carried to Mount Jackson, where I suppose they will give me an honorable trial. The Lieutenant and men appear to be gentlemen . . . . I am conscious of having acted the part

of a gentleman in returning the horses, I have the consolation of knowing I have faced death on a hundred battle fields, and should it be my sad lot to suffer death, I shall endeavor to die a brave man, and a gentleman . . . .

Remains of the Jacob D. Koontz House. While Jacob D. Koontz was able to make his escape, Newton Koontz was taken from this house by Federal troopers early before dawn on June 27, 1865. (From the author's collection)

To **Stop No. 28a**, proceed .1 miles to Shuler Lane (before the bridge) and turn left. This is the grade of the old Blue Ridge/New Market to Gordonsville Turnpike, along which Summers and Koontz were likely taken. Proceed .7 miles and look to your left to see the remains of the old Koontz-Shuler House. The Koontz family cemetery and final resting place of Sgt. Koontz is nearby.

Emma Jane Shuler, circa 1870
(Courtesy of John and Sandie Hammel)

Capt. Lycurgus D. Lusk. Captain Lusk took to heart the pleas of Summers and Koontz and went ahead to the camp at Rude's Hill to speak to Lt. Colonel Hussey before proceeding with the execution. (Courtesy of Philip D. Lusk)

The men are told of their fate

SMITH CREEK

Stop No. 64: Continue 1.8 miles to Rt. 340. Turn right and proceed 1.9 miles to Rt. 211. This is the old New Market to Sperryville Turnpike. Turn left and proceed 4.95 miles to Smith Creek. You have an opportunity to pull off briefly before crossing the bridge.

The Rochester Cavalry arrived at the foot of the Massanutten Mountain on the Shenandoah County side sometime during the afternoon of June 27 and Summers and Koontz were told that they were to be executed. Until that moment, no mention had been made by their captors of the requirements of Colonel Hussey's order and the young men pleaded for mercy. There was to be no trial, but the men were permitted to request the services of the local reverend, Socrates Henkel, for the last rites. Still the boys pleaded until they had somewhat convinced Capt. Lusk that the matter was a mistake. Taking his leave of the company, he rode on ahead to the camp to see what could be done.

On 22 May 1865, after the Civil War ended, Capt. George W. Summers, Sgt. I. Newton Koontz, and two other armed veterans of Co. D, 7th Virginia Cavalry robbed six Federal cavalrymen of their horses near Woodstock. The horses were returned the next day to the 192d Ohio Volunteer Infantry at Rude's Hill. Despite assurances that all was forgiven, Lt. Col. Cyrus Hussy, temporarily commanding the 192d, later ordered the men arrested. The others escaped, but Summers and Koontz were shot without trial here on 27 June. Thirty years later, Capt. Thomas J. Adams and friends erected the nearby monument to commemorate their deaths.

Summers-Koontz Marker and Monument. This monument marks the site of the execution on Rude's Hill, Shenandoah County. (From the author's collection)

The execution is carried out

"POST APPOMATTOX TRAGEDY" MARKER AND 1893 MONUMENT (RUDE'S HILL, SHENANDOAH COUNTY)

Sometime after Captain Lusk had departed, the detachment again started the march to the Federal camp. When within a hundred yards of the Federal bivouac, the company was stopped by a party of soldiers tasked with an on-the-spot execution. Summers and Koontz were permitted to write final letters to loved ones. Summers' note was simple:

> My Dear Father, Mother, Sisters, and Brothers:
> Very much to my surprise, we must soon leave this world to try the realities of an unknown one, but pray God that I had died upon the battlefield in defense of my dear native South! But it has been otherwise ordered. I submit to my fate. Pray for me, and try to meet me in heaven.

Newton Koontz wrote his fiancé and parents in two separate letters. To his "Darling Emma," he wrote:

> Oh, how can I bear to write you? Affliction is bearing me down! They are now ready to shoot me. Oh Emma, dearest in the world to me, how can I leave you but I must. Oh, I have heard you often say it would kill you to hear of my death. But dearest Emma take it as

To **Stop No. 65**, continue along Rt. 211 West for 1.4 miles to the town of New Market. Turn right on Congress Street/Rt. 11 and continue for 2.95 miles. There is a pull-off on the left near the Virginia Department of Historic Resources marker that was dedicated, like the one in Page County, on June 27, 1999

From the roadside marker, look into the field to see the monument that marks the exact spot of the execution. It was erected in 1893 by the efforts of Thomas Jackson Adams, a former member of Company K, 23rd Virginia Cavalry, and member of the Turner Ashby Camp, United Confederate Veterans. Adams had hoped that the site would be "often visited by those who admire courage and fortitude, and the tragic deaths of Capt. Summers and Sergt. Koontz will long live in the memories of our citizens and deserve to be recited in song and story, to show what atrocities our people suffered in war, and how heroically these men met their untimely fate."

Lt. Col. Cyrus Hussey, 192nd Ohio Volunteer Infantry (USAMHI.)

you can . . . . I wish to be buried with this ring on my finger. Emma, my respect to your father and mother whom I have loved as such, but no more.

To his parents he wrote:

I bid you all farewell in this world, hoping to meet you all in a better and happier world. I have been bandaged and tied to be shot, but have sent for Parson Henkel . . . . Remember dear ones that this world is all a shadow, only a moment in life, and death everlasting. Prepare to meet me in heaven every one of you, I will close . . . . I wish to be buried beside my dear mother. No more, goodbye forever.

Reverend Henkel may not have received the request as he did not arrive. At 7:30 P.M. the men were stood before a firing squad. Shortly thereafter they were riddled with bullets. In a postwar account from the 192nd Ohio, the conduct of the two condemned was "exemplary."

On the morning of June 28, the elder Summers showed up with his friends in order to defend the two men. But before the campsite was reached, and near 11 A.M., Summers found his son and Newton laid out on the ground with "stones for pillows. " Though the elder Summers had been a Unionist, he now felt a strong hatred toward the Yankees. He stated that he felt "cheated" out of the opportunity to influence the authorities. However, he later wrote, "To those that spoke evil and treated me unkindly I returned many kind acts."

On July 7 another party of 20 men under Lieutenant Henry E. Beeby, also of Company H, 22nd New York Cavalry, set out pursuant to Special Order No. 3, to apprehend and execute Jackson Kite and Daniel Koontz. Before the end of the day, orders from the Headquarters of the Army of the Shenandoah arrived calling for the action to cease. The two surviving men were pardoned by General Alfred T. A. Torbert, who, less than a year earlier, had carried out General Grant's orders to execute any of Mosby's men who were captured.

Daniel Fagan, Founder of Green Hill Cemetery
Fagan's service as first lieutenant of the Page Volunteers was brief.
Wounded at First Battle of Manassas and sick most
of the time thereafter, he resigned in May 1862.
In addition to his stonecutting and work organizing
Green Hill Cemetery, he was also once mayor of Luray.
(Courtesy of Terrence V. Murphy)

Begin **Tour No. 13** at the Luray-Page County Chamber of Commerce Tourism Information Center on Main Street in Luray. The tour is less than 2 miles in length and includes 5 stops at historic monuments and sites. All sites are located in Luray. Refer to the map on page 107 for assistance in locating the sites on this tour.

Turn right from the TIC parking lot and proceed east on E. Main Street for .2 miles to Green Hill Cemetery (**Stop No. 66**) on the right.

Legacy of a stone-cutter and Confederate veteran

GREEN HILL CEMETERY

IN 1877 STONECUTTER DANIEL FAGAN, A CONFEDERATE Veteran of the local "Page Volunteers," purchased the land here to lay out one of the most marvelous Victorian-era cemeteries in the county. Many Confederate soldiers and members of the Rosser–Gibbons Camp, Confederate Veterans, are buried here as well as many of the wartime political leaders of Page County, including Peter B. Borst, Mann Spitler, George W. Rust and others. Additionally, at

This early view of Main Street also gives a glimpse of the early days of Green Hill Cemetery which is just to the right. (D.L. Kauffman Post Card, from the author's collection)

least one Union veteran buried here; a former captain from the 66th Ohio Infantry who passed through Luray in 1862 en route to and retreat from Port Republic and later returning to be a successful merchant years after the war. Members of the Summers–Koontz Camp No. 490, Sons of Confederate Veterans, and Luray Chapter No. 436, United Daughters of the Confederacy, are also buried here.

By November 1877 Fagan had laid off the walks and drives. Additionally, "a great many of the trees have been set out and the varieties selected are the Cedar, Spruce, and White Pine. The taste displayed so far reflects credit upon its projector, Mr. Daniel Fagan, and when completed it will be an ornament to the town, as well as a great desideratum."

Through the early 1890s Fagan maintained a strong business that was well received by the community. In 1893 Fagan died and was buried in the cemetery that he had made possible. The cemetery holds not only Confederate veterans and political leaders, but also many people involved in the founding of Luray and Page County in the early nineteenth century.

Herbert Barbee's Confederate Monument

BARBEE MONUMENT

According to one source, the Herbert Barbee Confederate Monument was inspired by a visit by the sculptor to the battlefield at Gettysburg. While Union monuments were numerous, at that time, there was but one for the Confederate soldiers. Whatever the actual inspiration, Herbert Barbee got the idea for the pose from his youth. At some point, upon passing through Thornton's Gap or while near his father's birthplace at Hawsberry Inn near Panorama, Barbee saw a Confederate sentry standing in a snowstorm with the muzzle of his musket pointed down to keep the snow out.

Barbee Confederate Monument. This view of the monument was shot just one month after its dedication in 1898. (From a private contributor)

Stop No. 67 is .35 miles away on E. Main and Reservoir Streets. The monument will be on your left, but to obtain an optimal parking spot, you must enter into the shopping center lot.

The "Barbee" Confederate monument was sponsored by donations from private citizens throughout the South and even Northern states. Portraying a Confederate soldier without socks, shoes with holes, and tattered clothing, the monument differed from any other known. When placed on the outskirts of town prior to its dedication in July 1898, locals thought it an odd place. However, over time, the town of Luray has grown to encompass the monument within its limits today.

THE 1918 CONFEDERATE VETERAN'S MONUMENT

Though Luray already had the Barbee Monument on the east side of town, by 1912 veterans of the Rosser–Gibbons Camp, United Confederate Veterans, felt

Stop No. 68 is .8 miles away and along Cave Street. Turn left after the railroad tracks and enter the Railroad Depot parking lot. You may walk from here to the 1918 Confederate Monument.

Gathering of members of the Rosser-Gibbons Camp at the Confederate Veterans Monument in 1925 (From *Page: County of Plenty*)

130

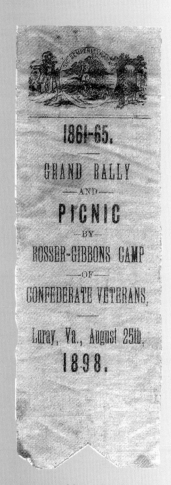

1861-65. GRAND RALLY AND PICNIC BY ROSSER-GIBBONS CAMP OF CONFEDERATE VETERANS, Luray, Va., August 25th, 1898.

Rosser-Gibbons Camp Reunion ribbon, 1898 (Courtesy of Coiner Rosen)

it necessary to raise funds for this monument. Local resident Frederick Taylor Amiss once wrote about the second Confederate Monument in Luray and stated that, prior to 1912, Lt. J. B. Seibert "was the originator and moving spirit" in the project. "Mr. Seibert's enthusiasm caused the Rosser–Gibbons Camp of Confederate Veterans . . . to take up the matter and it appointed a Monument Committee, with Mr. Seibert as Chairman" and Amiss as Secretary and Treasurer, "and selected from the Veteran Camp, the Luray Chapter of Daughters and the Sons Camp, others to make up the Committee."

While an initial inspiration in the project, Seibert died in the Fall of 1912. As a replacement chairman, former Mosby Ranger A. W. McKim was appointed.

Completed in November 1917 by the McNeil Marble Company of Marietta, Georgia, the monument was dedicated on July 20, 1918.

Though the intent was also to have plaques inscribed with the names of all loyal veterans from the county, funds were short and prevented the last phase of this project. Frederick Taylor Amiss, Commander of the local Summers–Koontz Camp No. 490, Sons of Confederate Veterans, went to great lengths to collect data on all of the men from 1913 until years after the monument's dedication.

A "Clasping of Hands"
The 1881 Reunion of Union and Confederate Soldiers

LURAY TRAIN DEPOT
National Register of Historic Places

Stop No. 69: After you return to the Railroad Depot parking lot, you will be in the area of the 1881 reunion of Civil War veterans. Actually, during 1881, a train depot was on the opposite side of the railroad tracks. The present historical depot dates to the first part of the twentieth century.

Having planned for a tour of the Luray Caverns in the summer of 1881, the Union veterans from the Captain Colwell Post No. 201 of the Grand Army of the Republic (G.A.R.) in Carlisle, Pennsylvania, also made arrangements to meet with Page County Confederate veterans and "have a general hand-shaking and expression of good feeling" with former foe. Within 12 days of sending invitations for

Luray Train Depot
This depot stood near the tracks in 1881
(Copy courtesy of Mike Salvino)

a reunion to "prominent men of Page County," a warm and friendly response was returned by local Confederate veterans.

When the G.A.R. Camp arrived in Luray at the Shenandoah Valley Railroad Depot on July 21 (the twentieth anniversary of the First Battle of Manassas), Confederate veterans were drawn up in military form in two files, with an evergreen arch on their right bearing the inscription: "In Union there is Strength."

After a series of speeches and the playing of the Star Spangled Banner, the two lines of men stepped forward and "clasped each other by the hands." The Carlisle *Herald and Mirror* reported: "During this part of the exercises many eyes were dim with tears of joy mingled with tears of sadness at the recollection of the dark days of war."

The procession of men and guests then moved onto the large dining hall of the Luray Cave and Hotel Company. When it came time to board the train again, "many were the regrets when the engineer whistled 'up brakes,' and all felt they must leave. Cheer after cheer went up as the train moved off from the station."

With such a warm reception received in Luray, the Union veterans agreed to invite the Page County Confederate veterans to Carlisle for a reunion on September 28 of that same year. "The citizens (of Carlisle) promptly furnished the money for the needed expenses."

Luray Inn. This photo by Silas K. Wright shows the inn about 1890. The Inn was owned by the Luray Cave and Hotel Company. (From the *Page News & Courier*)

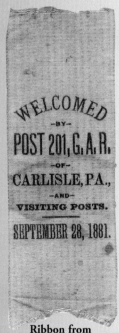

Ribbon from the 1881 Carlisle Reunion
(From a private contibutor)

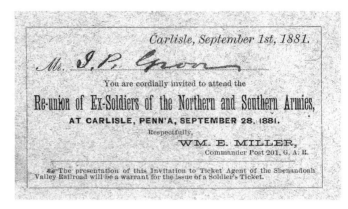

Train Pass for Page County Confederate Veteran John Pendleton Grove to attend the 1881 reunion in Carlisle. (Courtesy of Ann Vaughn)

To **Stop No. 70**, resume the driving tour and cross the railroad tracks. Turn right on Zerkel Street. You may park near the library

More than 200 veterans made the train ride with their families from Luray for a similar round of speeches and hospitality.

A Place for Comrades and reminiscing

INN LAWN PARK

Near the site of the old Luray Inn (which burned in the 1890s), this park became known for reunions of the local Confederate Veterans Camp. Large picnics and camaraderie between old war veterans was frequently shared on these grounds.

Named for Page County native Col. Simeon B. Gibbons (an aforementioned local and one-time commander of the 10th Virginia Infantry killed at the Battle of McDowell) and Gen. Thomas Lafayette Rosser (former commander of the Laurel Brigade), the Rosser–Gibbons Camp was originally organized as Camp No. 89 of the Grand Camp of Confederate Veterans. A July 1898 issue of *Confederate Veteran Magazine* mentioned the camp as having been organized in Luray, with sixty-seven members. On May 24, 1904, the camp was chartered as Rosser–Gibbons Camp No. 1561, United Confederate Veterans.

As an extension of the veteran's organization, both the Luray Chapter No. 436, United Daughters of the Confederacy and the Summers–Koontz Camp No. 490, Sons of Confederate Veterans, were formed and chartered in 1901 and 1904 respectively. Though they were dissolved for lack of members in the early twentieth century, they were revived and are still active in honoring Confederate veterans.

Due to the passing of many veterans and constantly thinning ranks, the Rosser–Gibbons Camp met for the last time as an organization in the spring of 1931.

The George W. Summers Camp No. 68, Grand Camp of Confederate Veterans was actually the first formally organized group of Confederate Veterans, and in fact, of war veterans in general, in Page County. Organized in Shenandoah, Virginia, in 1896 under the leadership of Robert S. Pritchett (commander) and J. E. Price (adjutant), the camp initially flourished and quickly established a United Sons of Confederate Veterans Camp, the Page Valley Camp No. 20. Leadership in Camp No. 20 included Real Sons E. L. Keyser (commander) and R. H. Cline (adjutant). Apparently never chartered as a United Confederate Veterans Camp, Camp No. 68 folded sometime before 1915.

A Confederate Memorial Day Celebration in Luray circa 1910 at the Grove Brothers Store, now the Luray Copy Service, near the present Tourist Information Center (Courtesy of Jo Ann Burner)

135

The Rosser–Gibbons Camp, Confederate Veterans, at a reunion in Luray Park, June 17, 1924. Union veteran James Wade LaConia also stands in the photo holding the U.S. flag.

(From the author's collection)

Bibliography

MANUSCRIPTS

Bridgewater College Archives, Alexander Mack Library, Bridgewater, Virginia Harry M. Strickler Papers

Handley Library, Winchester. John P. Louderback, typescript diary.

Library of Congress, Washington, D.C. Jedediah Hotchkiss Papers.

Library of Virginia Public Works Papers Pertaining to Turnpikes

National Archives, Washington, D.C. Barred and Disallowed Case Files of the Southern Claims Commission, 1871-1880. Compiled Service Records for Union and Confederate Organizations Morning Order Books for the 22nd New York Cavalry and 192nd Ohio Infantry

Page County Public Library, Luray, Virginia Genealogy and Local History Files

United States Military Academy Register of Graduates and Former Cadets

University of North Carolina, Chapel Hill, N.C. Kauffman, Joseph Franklin. Typescript Diary

Virginia Military Institute Archives, Lexington, Va. Alumni Records

NEWSPAPERS

Page Courier
Page News
Page News and Courier
Rockingham Register

PUBLISHED PRIMARY RESOURCES

Allan, William. *History of the Campaigns of Gen. T. J. (Stonewall) Jackson in the Shenandoah Valley of Virginia.* Philadelphia, 1880.

Armstrong, Richard L. *7th Virginia Cavalry.* Lynchburg, 1992.

____. *11th Virginia Cavalry.* Lynchburg, 1989.

Ballard, Charles C. *From Iron Plantation to Company Town: The Shenandoah Iron Works, 1836–1907.* Luray, 1998.

Baxter, Nancy Niblack. *Gallant Fourteenth: The Story of an Indiana Civil War Regiment.* Carmel, Indiana, 1980.

Baylor, George. *Bull Run to Bull Run: Four Years in the Army of Northern Virginia Containing a Detailed Account of the Career and Adventures of the Baylor Light Horse, Company B, Twelfth Virginia Cavalry, C.S.A.,* Washington, D.C., 1983.

Bonnell, John C., Jr. *Sabres in the Shenandoah: The 21st New York Cavalry, 1863–1866.* Shippensburg, Pa., 1996.

Brown, Peter A. *Mosby's Fighting Parson: The Life and Times of Sam Chapman.* Westminster, Maryland, 2001.

Brubaker, Mary S. *Mauck-Brubaker Families in the Page Valley of Virginia.* 1980.

Bureau of the Census. 1860; 1860. *Census records for Page County, Virginia.*

____. 1850; 1860. *Slave schedules for Page County, Virginia.*

Casler, John O. *Four Years in the Stonewall Brigade.* Guthrie, Oklahoma, 1895.

Collins, Darrell L. *The Battles of Cross Keys and Port Republic.* Lynchburg, 1993.

Confederate Veteran, 1893–1932.

Dabney, Robert L. *Life and Campaigns of Lieut. Gen. Thomas J. Jackson.* New York, 1866.

____. *Battle of New Market.* Garden City, N.Y., 1975.

Delaughter, Roger U., Jr. *18th Virginia Cavalry.* Lynchburg, 1985.

____. *McNeill's Rangers.* Lynchburg, 1986.

____. *62nd Virginia Infantry.* Lynchburg, 1988.

Denison, Frederic. *Sabres and Spurs: The First Rhode Island Cavalry in the Civil War, 1861–1865.* Central Falls, R.I., 1876.

Devine, John E. *35th Battalion Virginia Cavalry.* Lynchburg, 1985.

Dew, Charles B. *Ironmaker to the Confederacy: Joseph R. Anderson and the Tredegar Iron Works.* New Haven, Conn., 1966.

Douglas, Henry Kyd. *I Rode with Stonewall.* Chapel Hill, N.C., 1940.

Driver, Robert J., Jr. *First and Second Maryland Cavalry, C.S.A.* Charlottesville, 1999.

____. *The Staunton Artillery – McClanahan's Battery.* Lynchburg, 1988.

____. *The 1st and 2nd Rockbridge Artillery.* Lynchburg, 1987.

____. *1st Virginia Cavalry.* Lynchburg, 1991.

____. *5th Virginia Cavalry.* Lynchburg, 1997.

____. *14th Virginia Cavalry.* Lynchburg, 1988.

Dulfour, Charles L. *Gentle Giant: The Gallant Life of Roberdeau Wheat.* Baton Rouge, 1957.

Early, Jubal Anderson. *Autobiographical Sketch and Narrative of the War Between the States.* Philadelphia, 1912.

Evans, Clement A., ed. *Confederate Military History.* 12 vols. Atlanta, 1899.

Farrar, Samuel Clarke. *The Twenty-Second Pennsylvania Cavalry and the Ringold Battalion, 1861–1865.* Pittsburgh, 1911.

Fortier, John. *15th Virginia Cavalry.* Lynchburg, 1993.

Foster, Gaines M. *Ghosts of the Confederacy: Defeat, the Lost Cause, and the Emergence of the New South.* New York, 1987.

Freeman, Douglas Southall. *Lee's Lieutenants: A Study in Command.* 3 volumes. New York, 1942-44.

Frye, Dennis E. *2nd Virginia Infantry.* Lynchburg, 1984.

Gilmor, Harry. *Four Years in the Saddle.* Baltimore, 1986.

Goldsborough, William W. *The Maryland Line in the Confederate Army, 1861–1865.* Baltimore, Md., 1900.

Hale, Laura Virginia. *Four Valiant Years in the Lower Shenandoah Valley.* Strasburg, 1968.

Harris, Nelson. *17th Virginia Cavalry.* Lynchburg, 1994.

Heatwole, John L. *The Burning: Sheridan in the Shenandoah Valley.* Charlottesville, Va., 1998.

Henderson, William D. *The Road to Bristoe Station: Campaigning with Lee and Meade, August 1–October 20, 1863.* Lynchburg, 1987.

Hennessy, John J. *Return to Bull Run: The Campaign and Battle of Second Manassas.* New York, 1993.

Hewett, Janet B., et al., editors. Supplement to the Official Records of the Union and Confederate Armies. 100 vols. Wilmington, N.C., 1994 - .

Howes, Floyd. *Nauman-Norman Family History.* Privately published, 1965.

Huffman, James. *Ups and Downs of a Confederate Soldier.* New York, 1940.

Jessup, Harlan R. *The Painful News I Have To Write: Letters and Diaries of Four Hite Brothers of Page County in the Service of the Confederacy.* Baltimore, 1998.

Johnson, Robert Underwood and C. C. Buel. *Battles and Leaders of the Civil War.* 4 vols. New York, 1887.

Jones, Terry. *Lee's Tigers: The Louisiana Infantry in the Army of Northern Virginia.* Baton Rouge, 1987.

Kauffman, Charles Fahs. *A Genealogy and History of the Kauffman-Coffman Family.* Scottdale, Pa., 1940.

Kerkhoff, Jennie Ann. *Old Homes of Page County, Virginia.* Luray, Virginia, 1962.

Kidd, J. H. *Personal Recollections of a Cavalrymen with Custer's Michigan Brigade in the Civil War.* Grand Rapids, Mich., 1969.

Kleese, Richard B. *Shenandoah County in the Civil War: The Turbulent Years.* Lynchburg, 1992.

____. 23rd Virginia Cavalry. Lynchburg, 1996.

Krick, Robert K. *Conquering the Valley: Stonewall Jackson at Port Republic.* New York, 1996.

____. *Lee's Colonels: A Biographical Register of the Field Officers of the Army of Northern Virginia.* Dayton, Ohio, 1984.

____. *Stonewall Jackson at Cedar Mountain.* Chapel Hill, 1990.

Lake, D. J. and Co. *Atlas of Shenandoah and Page Counties, Virginia.* Philadelphia, 1885.

Layman, Kathryn Foltz. *The Christian Strole History, 1776–1983.* n.p., 1984.

McDonald, Archie P., ed. *Make Me a Map of the Valley, the Civil War Journal of Stonewall Jackson's Topographer, Jedediah Hotchkiss.* Dallas, Texas, 1973.

McDonald, William N. *A History of the Laurel Brigade.* Baltimore, 1907.

May, C.E. Life Under Four Flags in the North River Basin of Virginia. 1978.

Moore, Edward A. *The Story of a Cannoneer under Stonewall Jackson.* Lynchburg, 1910.

Moore, Robert H., II. *The Charlottesville, Lee Lynchburg, and Johnson's Bedford Artillery.* Lynchburg, 1989.

____. *Chew's Ashby, Shoemaker's Lynchburg and the Newtown Artillery.* Lynchburg, 1995.

____. *The Danville, Eighth Star New Market and Dixie Artillery.* Lynchburg, 1989.

____. *Graham's Petersburg, Jackson's Kanawha, and Lurty's Roanoke Horse Artillery.* Lynchburg, 1996.

____. *1st and 2nd Stuart Horse Artillery.* Lynchburg, 1999.

Murphy, Terrence V. *10th Virginia Infantry.* Lynchburg, 1989.

Musick, Michael P. *6th Virginia Cavalry.* Lynchburg, 1990.

Neese, George M. *Three Years in the Confederate Horse Artillery.* Dayton, Ohio, 1988.

Oates, William C. *The War Between the Union and Confederacy.* New York, 1905.

O'Ferrall, Charles T. *Forty Years of Active Service: Being Some History of the War Between the Confederacy and the Union and of the Events Leading Up to It.* New York, l904.

Martin, Samuel J. *The Road to Glory: Confederate General Richard S. Ewell.* Indianapolis, Indiana, 1991.

Miller, William J. *Mapping for Stonewall: The Civil War Service of Jed Hotchkiss.* Washington, D.C., 1993.

Musick, Michael P. *6th Virginia Cavalry.* Lynchburg, 1990.

Myers, Frank M. *The Comanches: A History of White's Battalion, Virginia Cavalry.* Baltimore, 1871.

Page County Bicentennial Commission. *Page: The County of Plenty.* Luray, Va., 1976.

Poague, William T. *Gunner with Stonewall.* Edited by Monroe F. Cockrell. Jackson, Tenn., 1957.

Rawling, C. J. *History of the First Regiment Virginia Infantry: Being a Narrative of the Military Movements in the Mountains of Virginia, in the Shenandoah Valley and East of the Blue Ridge During the War of Rebellion, of the First Regiment, Virginia Infantry Volunteers, Three Months' and Three Years' Service.* Philadelphia, 1887.

Reidenbaugh, Lowell. *33rd Virginia Infantry.* Lynchburg, 1987.

Reunions of Ex-soldiers of the North and South, held at Luray, Virginia, July 21, 1881, and Carlisle, Penn., Sept. 28, 1881. Carlisle, 1881.

Robertson, James I., Jr. *Stonewall Jackson: The Man, The Soldier, The Legend.* New York, 1997.

____. *The Stonewall Brigade.* Baton Rouge, 1963.

Salmon, John S. *The Official Virginia Civil War Battlefield Guide.* Mechanicsburg, 2001.

Shenandoah: *A History of Our Town and Its People.*

Sheridan. Philip H. Personal Memoirs of Philip H. Sheridan, General United States Army. New York, 1888.

Southern Historical Society Papers. 52 vols. Richmond, 1876–1919.

Starr, Stephen Z. *The Union Cavalry in the Civil War.* 3 vols. Baton Rouge, 1981.

Strickler, Harry M. Forerunners: *A History and Genealogy of the Strickler Families, Their Kith and Kin.* Harrisonburg, Va., 1977.

____. *A Short History of Page County, Virginia.* Harrisonburg, 1974.

Tanner, Robert G. *Stonewall ion the Valley: Thomas J. "Stonewall" Jackson's Shenandoah Valley Campaign, Spring 1862.* Garden City, New York, 1976.

Taylor, Richard. *Destruction and Reconstruction.* New York, 1879.

Thackery, David T. *A Light and Uncertain Hold: A History of the Sixty-Sixth Ohio Volunteer Infantry.* Kent, Ohio, 1999.

Thomson, Orville. *From Philippi to Appomattox: Seventh Indiana Infantry in the War for the Union.* Baltimore, 1993.

Tobie, Edward P. *History of the First Maine Cavalry, 1861–1865.* Boston, 1887.

U.S. War Department. *The War of the Rebellion: A Compilation of the Official Records of the Union and Confederate Armies.* 128 vols. Washington, D.C., 1880-1901.

Walker, Aldace F. *The Vermont Brigade in the Shenandoah Valley 1864.* Burlington, Vt., 1869.

Walker, Charles D. Memorial, Virginia Military Institute. Philadelphia, 1875.

Wallace, Lee A., Jr. *A Guide to Virginia Military Organizations, 1861–1865.* Lynchburg, 1986.

____. *5th Virginia Infantry.* Lynchburg, 1988.

Warner, Ezra J. *Generals in Blue: Lives of the Union Commanders.* Baton Rouge, 1964.

____.*Confederate Commanders.* Baton Rouge, 1959.

Wayland, John W. *A History of Rockingham County, Virginia.* Dayton, Virginia, 1912.

____. *A History of Shenandoah County, Virginia.* Strasburg, 1927.

____. *Stonewall Jackson's Way.* Verona, Va., 1969.

Weaver, Jeffrey C. *22nd Virginia Cavalry.* Lynchburg, 1991.

Wert, Jeffrey D. *From Winchester to Cedar Creek: The Shenandoah Campaign of 1864.* Carlisle, Pa. 1987.

____. *Mosby's Rangers.* New York, 1990.

Work Projects Administration Historical Inventory of Page County, Virginia. n.p., 1991

Worsham, John H. *One of Jackson's Foot Cavalry.* New York, 1912.

Index

143

About the Author

ROBERT H. MOORE, II, A NATIVE OF PAGE COUNTY, received his Bachelor of Science degree in Liberal Studies from Excelsior College in 1995 and completed masters classes in History at Old Dominion University. A ten-year veteran of the submarine force of the United States Navy, Moore has also been busy over the past fifteen years compiling the history of Luray and Page County in the Civil War. He has written seven books about twenty-nine Virginia artillery batteries for the Virginia Regimental History Series as well as articles for magazines such as *Civil War Times Illustrated, Blue and Gray Magazine* and *America's Civil War.* For the past five years, Robert has also maintained the "Heritage and Heraldry" column featuring the history and genealogy of Page County every other week in the *Page News and Courier.* Robert also serves on the History Committee for Virginia Civil War Trails and the Education and Interpretation Committee of the Shenandoah Valley Battlefields Foundation. He has served as chairman for the Page County Civil War Commission and is presently the Commander of the Summers–Koontz Camp No. 490, Sons of Confederate Veterans in Luray, tracing his lineage to at least six lineal Confederate ancestors who served in artillery, cavalry, and infantry units from Page County. Since 1997 he has played a role in securing funding and writing the text for eight of the nine Virginia Civil War Trails sites and one Virginia Department of Historic Resources marker in Page County. Robert is a member of the Virginia Association of Museums and the American Association for State and Local History. Robert is also a Freemason and member of the Ashlar Lodge No. 125 in Shenandoah. Robert and his wife reside in Augusta County, Virginia, with their two children.